Praise for *The Languages of Leadership*

The Languages of Leadership is a great tool for those who are keen to understand where they are in their leadership journey and how to shape their own brand and style as a connected and impactful leader.

Fiona Schutt, Chief Financial Officer, Worksafe Victoria

Ever had a boss who made you just want to switch off? "Blah, blah, blah…" When they talked in a meeting, you were more focused on not obviously falling asleep. Well, be different and don't be that boss.

This book written by Wendy Born is a great starter, reference and tool for leaders to be better. Be better at connecting. Be better at choosing the right words and behaviour.

Easy right? Nope. It isn't. It can be hard, very hard and that's okay because the gold is here in your hands.

Wendy talks about the Languages of Leadership. These are simple yet powerful concepts that I now use. They work. They make a difference. They are also as shallow and as deep as you'd like to go. She gets it. Her experience and the help that she offers is all captured here.

If you are an aspiring leader, please do not be the one blah, blah, blah-ing up front. Do it differently. Do it with purpose. Do it understanding and wanting to connect with those very people you lead. Do it with the right Languages of Leadership!

Digby Wilson, Principal, South East Australia, Field Service Delivery, Australia & International Delivery, Global Business Services, Telstra

Wendy manages to cut through to the essence of successful leadership. This book provides the tools to help you rethink your behaviours and practise effective leadership from within, whilst leveraging external elements to your advantage.

Anne Logan, Financial Controller Asia Pacific, Human Resources Manager Australia, MSX International

After leading large teams across a number of large organisations, and having the benefit of attending many leadership courses over the years, this book gave me knowledge, insight and challenged me with a fresh perspective. To be able to add these languages to my repertoire, and the knowledge to be able to apply the learnings in practical situations, means that this book isn't just about the theory that can't be applied. For this reason, it's a must-read book for any leader at any stage of their leadership journey.

Paul Harper, Program Director, Finance Business Transformation, Deakin University

We all have times when, as a leader, we feel stuck and are not getting the impact we want. Wendy's *The Languages of Leadership* provides a very practical guide to how you can take control of your words, actions and behaviours to become the leader you aspire to be. Whether you are new to a leadership role or a leadership veteran, there is something in this book for you. Take the time to invest in being the leader you aspire to be as 'your impact is your leadership footprint' and we all want to leave a legacy of footprints people are willing to follow!

Somone Johns, General Manager, Transformation, Telstra

Wendy has managed to define why language is so important in a simple and easy-to-read way. As a leader, I am constantly aware of how my language resonates with my team and this book explains why. The chapter on vulnerability is particularly relevant in today's business world, understanding why it is important to demonstrate vulnerability and how it builds trust within teams is brilliant.

Linda Barry, General Manager Programs, Alannah & Madeline Foundation

The Languages of Leadership is a book for all leaders at any stage of their career. Wendy provides practical tools and tips to help you to be a better leader for your people, have better relationships with your peers and to get noticed by your boss. Well worth the read.

Andrew McWhirter, CEO The Influencer Project

The LANGUAGES *of* LEADERSHIP

How to use your words, actions and behaviours to influence your team, peers and boss

WENDY BORN

MACMILLAN

First published in 2023 by Major Street Publishing Pty Ltd

First published in India 2023 by Macmillan
an imprint of Pan Macmillan Publishing India Private Limited
707 Kailash Building
26 K. G. Marg, New Delhi 110001
www.panmacmillan.co.in

Pan Macmillan, The Smithson, 6 Briset Street, Farringdon, London EC1M 5NR
Associated companies throughout the world
www.panmacmillan.com

ISBN 978-81-96365-39-4

1 3 5 7 9 8 6 4 2

Internal design by Production Works
Printed in India by Gopsons Papers Pvt. Ltd., Noida

CONTENTS

ABOUT THE AUTHOR

Wendy Born helps leaders maximise their talent and strengths to achieve extraordinary results.

As an engaging facilitator, coach, speaker (and now author) she works with executives, senior leaders and leadership teams to create high-performance organisations that deliver that WOW-factor.

On any given day, leadership can be rewarding, frustrating, fun, risky and scary – all within the first hour. It can make you feel annoyed, furious, happy, proud, inspired or like you want to curl up in a corner and rock back and forth.

With Wendy's guidance, leaders learn to build strong and enduring relationships to drive engagement and deliver on real strategic results that make the whole journey easier, more effective and, even, enjoyable.

Wendy is a highly experienced and recognised coach. She has more than 25 years of experience in corporate and management roles, including 10 years in senior leadership positions in finance, IT, retail, financial services, communications and government.

She also holds qualifications in human resources, finance, operations management and is a certified personal and professional coach. Plus, Wendy is a graduate from the Harvard Kennedy School, Executive Education in 21st Century Leadership.

When she's not working, Wendy is continually challenged by her two kids, Harry and Lucy, who (without knowing it) teach her more about leadership than you ever would think possible.

She would not have it any other way.

wendyborn.com.au
firstteamfirst.com.au

ACKNOWLEDGEMENTS

Few things in life are ever done in isolation. There is always a cheer squad in the background, helping, supporting and encouraging those who choose to pursue their passion. And so it is with this book. I have thoroughly enjoyed writing this, even though at times my brain hurt and doubts would creep in at 3am. So I would like to sincerely thank my cheer squad as follows.

Thanks firstly to my editor Kelly Irving for your guidance, advice and support and in particular your bottomless pit of patience. Your positivity and beautiful smile always encouraged me to keep going and reassured me that everything I was experiencing was normal! Thanks also to Lesley Williams and the team at Major Street Publishing – from the moment I met you I felt comfortable I was in good hands.

Thank you to my colleague Michelle Sales. Your friendship, along with your encouragement and support with my business and writing this book, has been invaluable to me and I will always be grateful to you.

Thanks to my best friend Alison Hawkins; you are always there when I need you. Your common sense, calmness and kindness continue to be a source of inspiration for me to be a better version of myself.

Thanks to Nicky Angelone, Ellen Horvat, Somone Johns, Dale Stevens, Digby Wilson and Graeme Crozier for your encouragement and allowing me to use your stories to bring the languages to life.

Thanks to my children, Harry and Lucy, for helping me to understand how leadership extends way beyond just our work lives.

And finally, thanks to you, the reader of my book. I hope this helps you to be the leader you want to be and your influence makes the world a better place.

INTRODUCTION

Sam is struggling at work. He's just been promoted to a new role as a senior leader in a large corporation and is in charge of leading about 3,000 people. The department is complex, running across the country with state-based general managers, who are in charge of their own smaller teams, now directly reporting to Sam.

Sam also has a new leader whom he dislikes, Rod. In trying to win the support of his new division, Rod has promised to fix a lot of problems, but there is much chatter around the organisation about whether Rod will actually be able to deliver anything at all. Rod's leadership style is significantly different to that of Sam's previous leader and many people are talking about him being inauthentic, narcissistic and tending to 'go rogue' and off-script, promising all sorts of unrealistic things.

He is worried that his team are expecting some of their big problems to be solved by Rod. If he doesn't deliver then the relationship between Sam and his people may be at risk.

Sam has also witnessed a lot of change in roles among his peers since Rod arrived, not to mention political games and passive aggressive behaviours. It is fairly common for people to go over heads, to escalate basic decision making and there's an overall lack of trust that people will deliver.

Then there's Sam's own leadership team. There are inconsistencies in the quality of service delivered across all of these teams ranging from outperformance to underperformance. The teams also tend to do things independent of each other, with little to no collaboration. They will agree to things in meetings and then do the opposite afterwards, and they all have differing views of what success looks like for their function.

Does this scenario sound familiar?

That's because it is. It's achingly familiar across many organisations in many different industries.

Many of us have issues trying to lead disparate teams with multiple personalities, colleagues with conflicting agendas and bosses with minds of their own.

The questions we often ask ourselves are:

- How do I manage my **team** leaders to work together without having to reinvent the wheel, to learn from and leverage each other's experience without getting competitive, and to be more effective in managing the performance of their own teams?
- How do I manage my **peers** to have productive and positive relationships, to make decisions more effectively without being dragged into the detail or office politics and to be more focused putting aside individual agendas?
- How do I manage my **leader** to stop making big promises to my team that I know they won't deliver on,

to give me the space I need to get my job done and to be open to my ideas and be willing to support them?

Once upon a time, it was enough just to lead your team and that was it. But organisations today are more complex, departments are vast, reporting structures are multi-faceted. As leaders, we are expected to manage so many different relationships at so many different levels in an organisation, that it can feel as if we need multiple personalities just to stay sane.

Even if you really like your job and the people you work with, there are so many things that need to get fixed. You can see the potential of the organisation, your function and your people, if only you could all get out of the way and get things done!

Any sort of progress is like pushing an A380 aircraft with your little finger – it's hard work, overwhelming and on the verge of breaking you.

If only you could get people on board with what you are doing. If only you could get the support you need from senior leaders. If only you could get your people moving in the right direction, together. If only…

The thing is that most of this 'stuff' is out of your control.

It doesn't matter how hard you try, how much you persevere, how much you try to control the behaviours of others, with this kind of approach you will still always feel stuck. You literally have no control over other people.

You don't have control over other people, but you do have control over yourself – your words, actions, behaviours... that is, your leadership language.

Managing relationships positively, effectively and productively starts with YOU.

There are six leadership languages you need to master to help you to manage anyone, anywhere:

- **I am an Active Leader**
  1. I am courageous
  2. I am strong
- **I am a Directive Leader**
  3. I engineer the world around me
  4. I abdicate power to others
- **I am a Perceptive Leader**
  5. I trust and am trusted
  6. I can be vulnerable.

I have worked with many leaders within some of Australia's largest organisations over the years, who have all been where you are right now. I have also been where you are now and I understand your frustration working for a leader who doesn't inspire you, and sometimes barely even notices you are there. I have worked with peers who actively seemed to work against me, and I've had team members who just didn't seem to care.

I have helped many leaders, just like you, overcome these obstacles by changing the way they talk and behave, because it's all within their control.

Sadly, we aren't taught this stuff in school, at work or on our MBA program. Instead, we often pick up the habits of those who have led us in the past or try and find a solution in a leadership book. The trouble is that a lot of information out there is focused mainly on the theory of leadership or leading people, but there is much more to leading than just theory.

You need simple, practical tools and techniques that you can action and implement everyday – that's what you'll find in this book. When you put all of these small changes together, that's when you get a big impact both individually and organisationally.

When you learn to balance these languages – and balance you shall soon see is the key – you start to get yourself noticed, to manage anyone at any level and to build your reputation in the market as one of the best leaders in your industry.

That's exactly what we're going to learn to do now.

Are you ready to learn the languages of leadership?

HOW TO USE THIS BOOK

Throughout my life I have always found that when I am learning something new, I need to watch someone else doing it first and then actually physically do it myself. This is the only way that I am truly able to master what I am learning. Then, the more I do it the better I get at it. Are you the same?

Whenever I work with a leader or leadership team, one of the first things I tell them is that I am a simple girl and complexity hurts my brain. So I will never give them anything complex or too hard to implement. Wherever possible I look for simple and easy ways to apply techniques and tools because if something's too hard it will never get done.

For these two reasons, I have designed this book to be a practical handbook for you to use. You'll find simple tools and techniques that don't take an age to practise, or hours and hours to master. Rather, they are simple and effective actions you can start taking today that will change how you lead, forever.

In Part I of this book, you will look at and understand the journey of leadership and how, when you reframe your thinking from blaming others to concentrating on what's within your control – your own words, actions and behaviours – your world opens up to allow you much more influence.

In Part II, you will be introduced to each of the six languages of leadership and find out how you can develop and put each one into practice when you need to. At the end of each chapter you will find words, actions and behaviours to actually practise using each language until you become comfortable with it.

Finally in Part III, you will learn how to balance each of the languages so you don't over or under use them, to avoid falling over.

There is nothing in the pages of this book that you can't ever do. You just need to take your first step, then your next and keep going.

As Benjamin Franklin once said: "Tell me and I forget. Teach me and I remember. Involve me and I learn."

So that's what we're going to do.

Part I

SPEAK THE TRUTH

Leadership is hard work. But most of the time, we blame everyone else for this!

The people we work with are always taking up so much of our time because they just can't get it right. They demand all of our focus and all of our attention.

We don't seem to have any influence or control over what is happening around us and we are frustrated, overworked and annoyed. We just can't seem to see the light at the end of the tunnel. We continue to be ineffective, losing credibility and unable to influence.

But the error in this reasoning is that we are surrounded by incompetence. It's everywhere, right? Except for with you that is.

So what if we started to shift our focus from what's actually going on, to what could be going on?

In Part I, you'll discover that we are better to reframe our own words, actions and behaviours instead of trying to control others.

You'll learn why it's easy to influence those around us, so that they do better things, become better leaders and achieve better results. Then, and only then, will you transform from being an isolated leader to an inspiring one.

Let's explore how.

In this part of the book, I help you understand why confidence plays such an important role in your leadership potential.

Chapter 1

I AM THE MASTER OF MY OWN DESTINY

"How's the new job going?" Simone asked.

"Oh terrible! I'm surrounded by idiots. You wouldn't believe it! The boss is all over my work and doesn't let me do anything outside the scope of my role. The people I work with are always questioning my decisions and then telling me how to manage my team. The people who work for me can't seem to get anything right and I am always having to step in and fix up their problems. I can't believe I took on this job in the first place" Peter replied.

"That sounds awful. What are you going to do?" asks Simone.

"Well, I can't do too much really, it's all down to everyone else, nothing's within my control. I guess I just have to live with it," Peter responded.

"Yeah, I know what you mean, it's the same everywhere".

When Peter got home that night his wife asked him how his day had been.

"Terrible, I can't work with these people, I have had to bring home a mountain of work to do because no-one around me seems to be able to do anything properly. I'm not sure how long I can keep doing everyone's job for them."

"Well, what about the parent–teacher meeting we have tonight, plus you said you would help the kids with their homework when we got home. When are you going to have time to do work?"

"Damn, I forgot. I'll have to do it all after the kids are in bed."

These types of conversations are all too familiar to leaders in an organisation, and they can cause a great deal of stress, both at work and at home.

You often find yourself doing everyone else's job, on top of your own, to make sure that work gets done and deadlines are met. The people who work for you seem to treat you like their parent, always asking for the answers to their problems, never being able to make a decision, and you have to sort out their fights like you are back in the playground.

At the same time, you're managing the delicate relationships with those above you, beside you and below you, just to get your job done.

You can't ever seem to get anywhere with your boss as they are either too controlling or you never see them. Your peers are like speed bumps on the road – they cause you to slow down considerably on what you see as a clear and straight path to your outcome. Sometimes if you go over them at high speed they cause damage to your suspension and can potentially knock you off course.

It's as if you're the meat in the sandwich, all the time.

As Peter says, you don't feel as though you can do much because it's *everyone else* who is impacting on your world. If they would just get out of the way, or get on board with what you are trying to do, your life would be so much easier. Right?

It's not your fault – or is it?

We are psychologically wired to believe that in scenarios like this it's everyone else who is at fault.

It is the psychological phenomenon known as the Fundamental Attribution Error that is at play here, helping you to lay the blame securely at everyone else's feet.

The Fundamental Attribution Error is defined by Mark Sherman Ph.D. in his article 'Why We Don't Give Each Other a Break' as "the tendency to overestimate the effect of disposition or personality and underestimate the effect of the situation in explaining social behaviour".

We are more likely to say that it is someone else's fault first before we consider the situation that contributes to that person's behaviour.

Here's an example to bring it to life.

Mary gets a promotion and in your eyes it's because she is just lucky, she sucks up to the boss all the time and is a know-it-all (her personality). It's certainly not because she has worked hard, closed a big deal and has had leadership experience before (her situation).

When we consider those we work with, we are more likely to explain their behaviour as a direct result of their personality, and certainly nothing to do with the situation that they are currently in. For example, that they may not be trained in something, that they have too much work to do, or they simply might be having a really bad day.

Fundamental Attribution Error also works in reverse, when it's always the situation that has impacted on us and is causing us to respond the way we do. It's got nothing to do with our own personality or behaviour.

We are also designed to take things personally which, despite being told many times over the years not to, most of us still tend to do!

As humans, taking it personally often drives many good things, such as our ethical behaviour, the way we manage risk and our overall work ethic. If we didn't take these things personally we would have a completely erroneous society.

In a *Harvard Business Review* article '"Don't Take It Personally" Is Terrible Work Advice', Duncan Coombe notes that when we don't take things personally we can become disengaged and indifferent. If we don't care enough we see fraud, workplace scandals and bullying start to increase.

Like most things, we also run the risk of taking things *too* personally leading to low self-esteem, stress and fear, and then we tend to overcompensate.

For example, Peter's need to take work home to compensate for his people not being able to do anything properly may be due to his fear of not meeting deadlines, or an excessive need for control of the outcome.

The key is to take your own work personally enough to stay motivated, but not so personally that you are offended or disheartened.

Circle of concern vs circle of influence

In Stephen Covey's best-selling book *The 7 Habits of Highly Effective People*, he talks about the circle of concern and the circle of influence.

In the circle of concern are the things you are concerned about yet have no control over, and in the circle of influence are all the things in your life you can control, or do something about.

By shifting your focus from your concerns, or things outside your control, onto things that are within your own influence, you find that your circle of influence becomes larger.

Conversely, if you are focusing on your concerns only, on that which you have little control over, you will find that your circle of influence shrinks.

The same can apply to how you manage the relationships you have with those you work with. Instead of focusing on everyone else, if you shift your focus onto that which you can control – namely your own behaviours – you may find that your influence and impact over those you work with will increase.

Understanding the influence that your own behaviours have on those around you is an attribute of Emotional Intelligence (EQ). The link between Emotional Intelligence and effective leadership is well documented and leads to increases in productivity, motivation and engagement.

In Daniel Goleman's book *Emotional Intelligence*, he talks about the value of EQ for fostering good social interactions because it helps you to empathise more through better understanding of the situations of others. There is nothing more valuable than walking a mile in another person's shoes.

It therefore makes sense that understanding more about how your own behaviour is contributing to the circumstances and people around you, and how that flows back to impact your life, can lead to an increase in understanding and further empowering you to have more control over your circumstances.

In his book *Vital Friends: the people you can't afford to live without*, Tom Rath found that where people have positive relationships at work, or even a best friend, they are seven times more likely to be engaged in their job and be more productive.

Additionally, when writer Chris Bailey decided to do an experiment on productivity strategies by isolating himself for ten days from friends and family in the basement of his girlfriend's father's house, he discovered that his motivation to get work done reduced significantly, and that the primary reason he was working was for the benefit of the people he loved.

Increasing our circle of influence, and decreasing the impact of the Fundamental Attribution Error, therefore enables us to take things personally in a positive way that actually drives our performance.

Reflect on how you can change

I once worked with a guy who constantly said he was 'the numbers guy'. He believed that this was an adequate rationale for him not to have to deal with any personal issues with his people. This was simply 'who he was' and he used this as an excuse not to change anything! (I'm sure you know someone like this… maybe it's even you, if you're being honest.)

Neurologically our brains are wired to put us on autopilot, which means we will always behave in a way that is in-built to us; to do what comes naturally to us, which has been developed over many years, influenced by things like our education, parental influence, socio-economic factors, values and beliefs.

The problem with being on autopilot is that we rarely take the time to listen to what we are saying, or reflect on what we have done, to be able to draw insight from these actions in order to understand them.

If we don't understand what we are doing, we have no chance of changing it to get a better outcome.

Regular reflection of our words, actions and behaviours has a positive impact on our overall wellbeing. Meier, Cho and Dumani (2015) in the *Journal of Organizational Behavior*, found that "work reflection was associated with an increase in affective wellbeing, with regard to both positive and negative moods." Additionally, research conducted by Stefano et al on call centre productivity found that those employees who reflected on their performance for 15 minutes each day performed 23% better than those who didn't reflect.

If reflection has such a positive impact on our overall wellbeing and performance, why is it that so few of us actually do it?

Reflection can be confronting, because it means looking at what we have done, which isn't always good. It means that we may have to admit that some of the things we do aren't really that nice and don't contribute to the greater good. This makes us uncomfortable and vulnerable, and we tend to avoid doing it.

In Jennifer Porter's article in the *Harvard Business Review*, 'Why you should make time for self-reflection (even if you hate doing it)', she concludes that leaders often don't understand the process, don't like the process, don't like the results, have an over-bias towards action rather than thinking, and can't see a good return on investment from reflection.

Taking the time to reflect on our actions and how they impact others gives us an opportunity to create meaning, and from meaning comes learning.

Learn to lead better

Reflection needs to be part of your daily routine, something that you take the time to do without fail, and if you miss doing it your day isn't finished. This is a critical leadership activity that will lead to a continual loop of improvement for you – but only if you commit to a regular practice. Continuing to improve the way you do things leads to better relationships with those you lead, those you work with and those you report to. This leads to better productivity and to better bottom lines for organisations.

Through creating this continual learning loop, you become the leader you want to be. You continue to make tweaks and adjustments to what you say and do, which are observed by those you work with. They see you kicking goals, winning deals, influencing those around you and your confidence growing. They want to come and work for you, be led by you and be inspired by you. You are more in control of where you are going, what you want to get done, and you're doing it on your terms.

You're the master of your own destiny – so own it.

Change is within your control

Andrew was the General Manager of an operations function with a large organisation. He had seven direct reports who had varying degrees of competence and experience. Andrew was a control freak, and he managed each one of his direct reports like pawns in a chess game.

He would often talk to members of his leadership team about other members, as if 'comparing notes'. He kept everyone on their toes with his volatile behaviour; his team never knew what mood he was going to be in, he would switch in a matter of seconds from being nice guy to nasty guy, tearing the paint off the walls with his verbal tirades.

This led his leadership team down a path of dysfunction, having to manage up well or be eaten alive. The culture within the business unit was one of name, blame and shame to cover your backside at all costs. They were all for their own self-interest and this permeated down throughout the function. Things were grim, engagement low and everyone was trying to get out.

When Andrew was promoted to another role in a different area of the organisation, his natural replacement was one of his direct reports, Chris. Chris had been in the function for a little over 12 months, and was considered to be a high-potential employee.

Chris had come from outside the organisation and had a broad range of experience leading large teams. His experience of being led by Andrew had disappointed him, and he knew the team were in a bad way. He knew he had a lot of work ahead of him to rebuild the team.

Chris took the team away on an offsite and told them how his personal reflection of his own behaviour over the last 12 months had led him to believe that he could have done more to support the team under Andrew's leadership. He felt there were times when, as a senior leader within the team, he had acted in a selfish way and was more concerned about his own function instead of the whole team. He told them he planned to lead in a very different way to Andrew and would value their help and support to lead the function. Chris considered the team to be his work family and wanted the team to start building their trust with each other, so they could all feel supported and appreciated for what they achieve.

Twelve months after Andrew had left, the team are now in a very different place. They are still a work-in-progress, however by learning from the past, reflecting on their own behaviour and building trust within the team, they are managing to deliver more of their targets than previously.

Chapter 2

I CAN TRANSFORM FROM ISOLATED TO INSPIRING

Adrian's leadership team was in disarray. Over the past two years they had experienced a significant amount of change, including changes to leadership as well as new appointments to their team.

Everyone was used to operating in silos, focusing on their own individual business units, and they rarely collaborated on anything. There was no focus on the collective team and what they could achieve together. The team seemed to coast along finding it difficult to reach consensus or make decisions.

They had defined their team behaviours and values, yet they weren't actively living them. There was a lack of defined communication standards, which led to their inability to raise concerns or engage in conflict without fear of repercussions.

Trust existed within pockets of the team and there were unspoken norms about how to engage with each other, but overall the team was dysfunctional.

Adrian knew there were problems. He felt there was a lack of vision for where the team wanted to get to but didn't know how to bring everyone together to create it. He knew there were trust issues, hell… he himself didn't trust half of them!

There was also feedback coming from stakeholders outside the business unit that the people who reported to his leadership team were behaving in the same way. They were obviously seeing how their bosses behaved and following their example.

Adrian knew he was running out of time to get this together because there was mounting pressure from his stakeholders and customers to fix things, and his boss's and the team's reputation was losing ground. He was angry, frustrated and felt the only way to create some kind of urgency was to perform a stunt or two. If he turned off a system, or let a big deadline slip, that would get their attention and then they might act. He was desperate.

When I worked with Adrian and his team to try and turn some of these challenges around it was tough! Initially he came across as too harsh, he had limited self-awareness and couldn't see the big picture let alone define it. Then one day a small glimmer of vulnerability arose.

The team needed help – and for the first time they were able to admit it.

The next 12 months kicked off with an offsite because the leadership team needed to be away from their environment in order to be given the hard truth about what was going on. There was data to show they were dysfunctional, their words proved their care factor was low, and their actions demonstrated there was a lack of confidence from their people. They didn't like it. It was hard for everyone in the room. They knew it was the truth.

As the team accepted their mistakes and that they were the only people who could control or change them, they started to share things about themselves, parts of their lives that they had never shared with their colleagues before. This showed their colleagues that they were individuals.

Then they started to take risks, small at first, that required them to draw on their courage and strength. They learned to trust each other by being vulnerable together – taking the simple, yet not easy, step of asking for help. They learned that sometimes they needed to be tough with each other, to have hard conversations and call out elephants in the room when they needed to. They called each other out, they stood up, they stood out and they stepped up.

They worked hard on building themselves as a team, and building the confidence of their people, over the 12 months. They didn't always get it right, but they were quick to acknowledge when they didn't and to promptly set a course to correct.

Their stakeholders started telling them how they had seen significant change and that they were easier to do business with.

This group of leaders had to shift their own mindset to actually get the change they wanted. Not everyone survived the journey. Some left of their own accord, others were moved on, the majority remained though. They all had their own idiosyncrasies which had to be accepted or changed to enable the team to move forward. But everyone agreed that it wasn't about any one individual, it was about the team.

When your words, actions and behaviours are aligned to wanting to work together, wanting the best for the team or organisation, and wanting the best for those you lead, you find that you see progress with your work, you hear words and phrases that are more positive and you feel more engaged with what you are doing.

When you shift your focus from what you can *get* to what you can *bring* you become more effective both as a single entity and as part of a team.

What you focus on, grows

Tony Robbins, author, entrepreneur and philanthropist has famously been quoted as saying that "where focus goes energy flows" and I have seen this play out time and again in organisations. When leaders focus on a particular area of their business, things start to change. Daniel Goleman believes that a leader's focus of attention directs and guides the attention of those he or she leads, providing a ripple effect across the organisation.

When you focus on changing your own words, actions and behaviours, all the things that you can control, you will find that your people will notice this about you, and you will start to impact positively on them.

This then permeates throughout your team, function and organisation and you will find that the same positive shift starts to happen in others.

Just take a moment to think about all the best leaders you have worked with in the past. Now think about your own leadership. Do you see any similarities? I expect that you do, because we tend to mimic those around us. If you stay in a culture that is negative for long enough, you will start to change your behaviours to align to it. (I'm sure you've been in an organisation like that at some point.)

According to neuroscientist, Marco Iacoboni, our brains have a neuron called the mirror neuron, which helps us to recognise the people we know, to understand facial expressions and copy the behaviours of others. It makes us yawn and laugh when we see others yawning and laughing. He believes that "mirror neurons… provide some kind of inner imitation of the actions of other people, which in turn leads us to simulate the intentions and emotions associated with those actions".

So, if this neuron is active in all of our brains we should use it to our advantage.

If all we have to do is yawn to get someone else to yawn, surely other behaviours we exhibit can be just as easily influenced.

The six levels of leadership

Let's think about this in relation to where you are in your organisation today. There are six levels of influence that you could possibly have on those around you, as shown in Table 2.1.

Table 2.1: The six levels of leadership

Level	Activity	Result	Value
6	Inspired	You're on fire	+100
5	Influenced	You know your way around	+70
4	Integrated	You're kicking some goals	+50
3	Involved	You get the job done	0
2	Interested	You may get left behind	-20
1	Isolated	You're sitting in a silo	-50

Each level will have an impact on you, your boss, your peers and your people. When you understand each level you are able to identify where you currently sit, so that you can then start to put things in place to move up and increase your value to your team, function and organisation along the way.

Let's explore each level in detail.

Level 1 – Isolated

If you are isolated then you are sitting in your own nicely developed, insular, fortress-like silo. It's akin to being in Fort Knox, and it's nicely controlled by you as its king or queen.

You work primarily with your team, protecting your patch and watching your back. You don't trust too many people except those you have groomed nicely to protect you.

You are likely to be very political, manipulative, and when you do get things done you leave a mountain of collateral damage in your wake. You get noticed by senior leaders either because you are managing them well, or because they don't like you at all!

Level 2 – Interested

When you're interested then you are a bit hit-and-miss on delivery. Your people have mixed feelings about working for you – some love you, some don't.

You may have a seat at the table with your peers, or your stakeholders, but you have minimal impact while you're there. You don't get taken seriously because you're either seen as a threat or a force to be reckoned with, which means your peers have limited respect for you. Senior leaders may ask "who's she?", but not necessarily for good reason.

Level 3 – Involved

If you're involved then you're good at getting the job done. You're a solid performer and usually get scored in the middle of the range in your annual performance review.

You are a team player, and your peers respect you for that, but your name's not showing up in lights. You can often take on too much, usually because your peers have kept quiet knowing you will volunteer to do the work. This can mean you also sometimes get taken advantage of because you're a good loyal employee.

Level 4 – Integrated

When you're integrated then you are working beyond your remit, across the function, collaborating with your peers and getting things done.

You are probably seen as talent with potential in the next five years. However, although you are promised more challenging jobs or opportunities, they never really come to you. There is always some reason as to why: someone else had more experience than you; you were the second choice because…

The work you are doing is valuable and you are kicking some goals but not consistently. You are a loyal employee, you want to progress, and you are desperate to get noticed by the right people.

Level 5 – Influenced

Once you arrive at 'influenced' then you are getting work done across and outside of your business unit. You are an active collaborator, and you have great relationships with your peers inside and outside of your business. Your bosses and colleagues know exactly who you are and often tell you that they have a job for you when you're ready to move.

You are starting to earn a reputation across the organisation as someone who works hard and will go far.

You are a great networker and can navigate your way through the appropriate channels to get things done. You are considered talent with potential in the next two years.

Level 6 – Inspired

Now you're inspired you have solid relationships with senior leaders across the organisation and this includes the CEO.

You actively network both inside and outside your organisation, and you have a reputation for being innovative within the industry. You are considered talent with the potential to be top dog one day.

You have a team of people who are loyal and inspired by your work, they have the highest respect for you. You are in the trenches beside your people when you need to be, you value and support them even when they fail, and they know you have their backs, as they have yours. You're on fire.

Now ask yourself: Where do you see yourself now and where do you want to be?

Levelling up

If you're like most people, you obviously want to get to level six as a leader.

But as Adrian and his team discovered, moving up takes time, commitment and focus. It's a journey for you, your team and your people – that you all go on together.

When you commit to this kind of endeavour you find that you actually buy back more time to focus on the strategic and broader issues that you really should be focusing on as a senior leader. You stop fighting fires and start to find the courage you need to take more risks.

You connect with your people and create a work family that has each other's backs, that looks out for each other, that cares about each other, that works as a team and that achieves great things. You have better quality relationships with your boss and your peers, and you build your presence. Your circle of influence continues to grow.

When you inspire your people to step into their roles and to be more deliberate with their own actions, behaviours and words, you will find that they start to lead your business for you.

Isn't that what leadership is all about?

Step into your standard

Sadly, there are usually only one or two leaders we work for over our entire career that we would drop everything to work for again. You know the type. When you think about them, you know they changed your life. When you hear their name you automatically think about how great they were to work for. If they rang you tomorrow and offered you a job, you would start typing up your resignation letter to hand in to your current employer.

When Michelle first offered me a job, the fact that I had little experience in what she was looking for wasn't lost on me. I was so grateful for the opportunity she gave me that I made sure that I didn't let her down in any way. She had taken a risk and my goal was to make sure it paid off for her.

I got to know the other members of the team I was in. They were a great bunch of girls for many reasons. They were calm under pressure, maintaining the confidence of their stakeholders no matter what the circumstances. They knew their stuff and were considered to be the experts in their chosen field by their customers. Everyone engaged in robust debate about key issues when they arose, and respected the decisions made by the team, even though at times it wasn't what some of them wanted. They supported each other, challenged each other and felt supported by Michelle with everything they did.

As I watched Michelle lead the team I noticed how her leadership style was different to what I had been used to in the past. It was clear to me she was an inspiring leader. Over time, it occurred to me that the reason the team was like this was because of the way Michelle was.

Michelle would challenge when needed, was calm and confident in all her interactions, and she was respected by everyone who came into contact with her. She supported every member of the team and showed this through her words and actions.

It was clear that Michelle's leadership had set the standard, and her team were stepping into that standard.

Part II

ACT OUT THE LEADERSHIP LANGUAGES

When you take ownership of your own words, actions and behaviours then you stop feeling isolated from everyone and start to inspire those around you. When you feel inspired about things, you start to be more productive, you become more focused on the right things, you start to feel great about the work you are doing, and you start to encourage those around you to do the same.

But the question is: How?

How do you change your own words, actions and behaviours to influence those around you, to influence results and to lead productive teams with less hassle, less politics and less drama?

In Part II, we explore the six languages of leadership that you need to adopt, depending on the situation that arises:

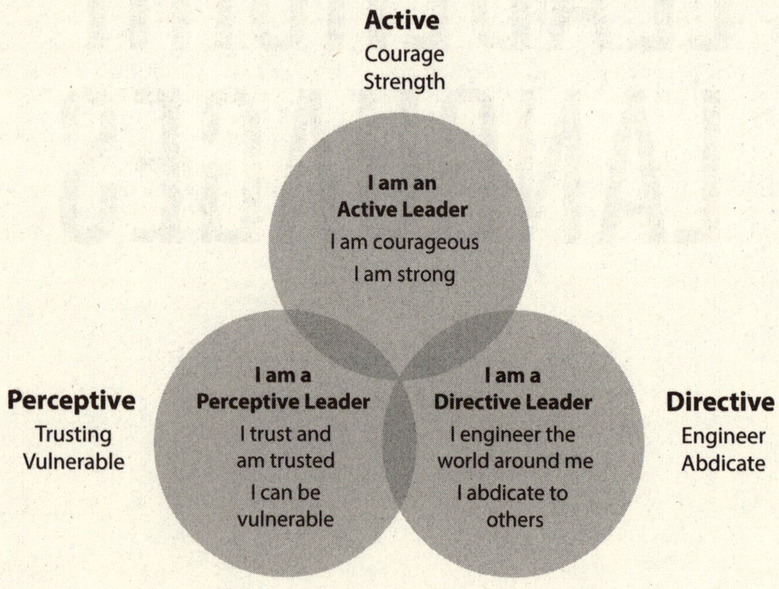

We'll look in detail at examples of each and unpack where you're at now – how fluent you are in each leadership language – and where and how you can improve to become a more influential leader.

Let's begin by exploring the Active Leader and the languages of courage and strength.

I AM AN ACTIVE LEADER

I am courageous

I know that being scared witless about something is no reason not to do it. I am not afraid to start something before having all the answers because I know I am resourceful enough to think on my feet and come up with solutions. If I fail, I will survive and I always learn something valuable from the process.

I am strong

I am able to make tough calls when I need to. I can call out something important, that is being left unsaid in the room, even if it makes people uncomfortable. I stand up for what I believe in and fight for the right thing. I push my people to stretch and deliver, always with respect, fairness and dignity.

Chapter 3

I AM COURAGEOUS

In the 1980s movie *Working Girl*, Melanie Griffiths plays the role of Tess a working girl from Brooklyn, New York. Frustrated with being played a fool by her bosses, she gets her revenge by publicly insulting them – before being fired.

Tess lands a new role as a secretary to Katherine Parker, where she is encouraged to share her ideas with Katherine – there's 'an open door' policy between them. Tess, feeling comfortable that Katherine has her back, shares her killer idea about a client, which Katherine then passes off as her own!

When Tess discovers Katherine's plan to use her idea, she goes to executive Jack Trainer, played by Harrison Ford, for help. A rollicking ride with many confrontations ensues, culminating in Katherine having to 'fess up to what she has done and Tess being offered her dream job with the client.

It took a great deal of courage and determination by Tess to pull this off. The catalysts for her actions were her humiliation, disappointment and frustration with not getting anywhere. Sadly, it often takes something like this to really upset us before we will actually tap into our courage and do something about it.

Courage is something that we all have, yet sometimes struggle to show to the world.

Fight, flight or freeze?

Often, we surprise ourselves when courage turns up. We reflect on it afterwards as something completely unexpected that we didn't realise we had!

It can also be quite uncomfortable for those who show courage and those who witness it, which is probably the main reason we often think twice before using it.

There are different types of courage, of course, all very much dependent on the circumstances and nature of the risk that appears. For example, the level of courage required to save someone from a burning building is not really the same as that needed to call out a colleague or boss behaving badly. Or is it?

To our brain, courage happens in response to a real or perceived threat. When we experience this threat or fear, we have a neurological reaction, stemming from prehistoric times when our sole purpose was to try and stay alive and not be eaten by other animals.

Our amygdala, the little almond-shaped section of nervous tissue that sits in the limbic part of our brains responsible for our emotions, instincts and memory, goes into overdrive creating a chemical cocktail of adrenaline and cortisol. This triggers the fight, flight or freeze action required to keep us alive.

When this happens, the cerebral or pre-frontal cortex part of our brain, which is responsible for our sensible, rational thinking, shuts down and we are unable to think straight. That's why it's not until three hours later when we have calmed down that we can think of a million smart, witty things to say or do.

It doesn't matter if someone comes at us with a knife or someone says something nasty to us, we have the same neurological reaction. This is why we don't like to be courageous, because our brains perceive we may die from the experience.

It's easy to get scared and flee, it's harder to stay and fight.

What's your fear?

In her book *Brave*, Margie Warrell talks about the importance of fear in our lives. She tells us that it is part of our DNA, designed to protect us (from the hungry predators, remember?). Yet in today's world, most of our biggest fears are in our head and made up of non-life-threatening challenges such as a fear of public speaking, fear of change, fear of being judged, fear of being alone and many more.

If this fear isn't managed or controlled it can take over your life, reduce your confidence, increase your stress and anxiety and keep you from doing anything outside of your comfort zone.

At work, fear prevents you from challenging the status quo, looking for ways to do things differently, being creative in your solution-finding and it means you won't support your people when they stuff up or have a brilliant idea. In a nutshell, you won't go anywhere.

With access to so much information via the media, social media and on the internet in general, we are constantly being bombarded with information – mostly negative – that is designed specifically to create fear. The result of this is that we are more likely to feel unsafe, a victim and suffer from increased anxiety.

At work we are constantly in fear of retribution, being humiliated, being judged and being stuck where we are, forever.

Is it any wonder we feel uncomfortable being courageous? It's much easier to stay safe, secure and where we are.

Sometimes it's actually fear itself that we are afraid of. We are scared of feeling scared because it makes us really uncomfortable. If it gets out of control, fear can be all-consuming and can get in the way of us achieving great things or reaching our full potential. Fear will stop us from leading our people the way they want to be led, or the way they deserve to be led.

If you give in to fear, you will limit your influence, have less control over the things you deal with every day and your life will be harder and even more stressful. Now does that sound like any kind of leader?

Turn fear into flight

I once went to a hypnotist to help me get over my fear of flying. Even the thought of getting on a plane would cause me to break out in a sweat and my heart would race, and I would catastrophise that if I got on the plane I would be the victim of Australia's first major domestic airline tragedy. No-one could tell me any different.

This fear was so paralysing that it wasn't until my clients wanted me to travel interstate that I realised I had to do something about it. I simply could not afford to put my most valuable relationships at risk because of my fear of flying.

The thing I learned from the hypnotist was that fear was something ingrained in my everyday life, like an old friend. If she hypnotised me about my fear of flying, I would just shift the fear to something else in my life. So she asked me if I would like to be able to manage fear in a more proactive way rather than letting it control my life.

Honestly, I had to think about it. This would need me to be courageous and to let go of stuff – stuff I had been lovingly nurturing for years, my security blanket. Did I have the courage to do it?

I am happy to say that I did. I found that courage is kind of like a muscle, you can stretch it and work at it to build it up and sometimes even make it up as you go along.

Mark Twain once said, "Courage is resistance to fear, mastery of fear – not absence of fear." I was able to find a different way to do things, even though I was scared of what might be on the other side.

If you aren't courageous, then your world won't change.

Shining a light

Fear can keep you put down, shut down and toned down. But when you bring it out into the open and shine a light on it, you realise that it's not just *your* fear, others have it too. It then gets smaller, you get to look at it, analyse it and sometimes even laugh at it.

Whatever your fears are, you can work through them to overcome them. We are lucky because at work we are rarely in a life-or-death situation that requires enormous courage, so we can actually anticipate a lot of the situations we may encounter. For example, standing up to your boss when you disagree with him or her, calling out your peers when they are acting in an inappropriate manner, delivering difficult messages to your people, calling out elephants in the room, managing performance, etc., are all challenges that come up every day in our working lives.

These aren't unique situations, so they provide you with a distinct advantage of being able to prepare for them.

You can actually practise or script how to cope with these situations to help your brain recall the words in the future, making it a little easier to respond than if you had been caught off guard.

If your fear is really bad, then you can employ exposure therapy. This is a psychological treatment used to help people to manage their fears through gradual and continual exposure to them over a period of time. The aim is to get you used to dealing with your fears, so that the stigma attached to them will eventually reduce.

For example, in the 1960s, the civil rights movement in America used exposure therapy to help students to peacefully protest against black segregation in Nashville. Workshops on the philosophy, tactics and techniques of non-violence were held by students prior to a sit-in or demonstration to help them to manage their fear and the responses they would likely encounter from members of the community once the protests began.

By being exposed to these responses over a number of workshops the students were then able to manage their fears effectively, along with the responses they encountered, and this meant they could hold their ground. Three weeks after the commencement of their protests they were successful in having black customers served at lunch counters across Nashville.

By practising courage, when the situation presents itself, you'll be scared but you will definitely be better prepared.

Reflect and rewrite

Another way to shine a light on fear is through reflection and writing. Taking time each day to reflect and write about things that went well and things that worried us, is a great habit to get into as it helps the continual loop of learning from what we are doing.

By reflecting on what things you feared today, or what stopped you from doing what you wanted, you can help bring your fears out into the open.

That way you can look at them, examine them, and understand them a little bit better. It also helps you to understand exactly what it is that you fear and put a label on it. If you can label your fear you have a much higher chance of reducing the effect that it has on you physiologically (the amygdala reaction) and a better chance of controlling your reaction.

Remember to breathe.

Being aware of your physiological reaction to fear, right before you need to decide whether to be courageous or not, will help you to better manage your response.

Remember how the cerebral part of your brain shuts down while your amygdala is going to town? That's what stops you from having the choice to be courageous, causing your fight, flight, freeze response. Navy SEALs use a 4X4 method of deep breathing while they are in conflict to manage their response. This involves breathing in through your nose for a count of four and then breathing out through your mouth for a count of four. If you can, do this three times, immediately after you become conscious that you are reacting. It will help you to re-engage your pre-frontal cortex and respond more rationally and courageously.

When we are able to shine a light on the fears that we have and bring them out into the open, we gain the opportunity to understand them more, look at them objectively, share them with other people, and overcome them so that we can then practise being courageous.

It's only by being courageous that things in our life will start to change.

It's contagious

When we are courageous at work we send a strong message to those around us that we are confident, in control and will lead by example. We show that we have values and we are willing to stand up for what we believe in. Courage is also contagious and you will find that once you start being courageous, others will too.

By being courageous in your role you are aiming to create a culture of openness and honesty and living the values that you and your organisations espouse. You are looking to influence change within your team, your function and your organisation by actively leading the way for those around you.

Showing courage is hard work, uncomfortable and difficult, but actions always speak louder than words. Practising courage every day shows those you lead that it is OK to stand up for what you believe in, to stand out from everyone else, and to lean into discomfort. It shows those you work for that you value integrity and ethical work standards. And it shows those you work besides that you are a supportive and solid peer.

Stand up and stand out

Ellen was a senior leader in a large bank. Her role was strategic in nature and she was very good at what she did, yet she lacked the ability to confidently stand in front of the executive team and the board to present her work.

When she thought about talking to an executive, Ellen's heart rate would increase, her breathing would become shallow and her palms get sweaty. She said more often than not that her mind would go blank, and when she was able to think she would stumble over her words, and if she was questioned she would start to second guess herself and question her ability.

Ellen's amygdala was being hijacked and she was panicking, so we worked on her breathing. We practised some deep breathing techniques and I asked Ellen to take three deep breaths before she started speaking, the next time she was in front of the executive. This helped Ellen to stay calm and keep her pre-frontal cortex working, and she was able to think clearly and answer calmly.

Next, we worked on Ellen's confidence. We spoke about all the times in the past when she had got things right, and there were many – many more than the times that she had got it wrong –

and the few times when she had got it wrong, we realised that the world didn't end, her fears weren't realised and she actually learned a great deal from the experience. This helped Ellen to shine a light on her fears and to move past them.

Ellen has now moved on to another role at a higher level with much greater responsibility. She works with a new executive team every day and is considered by them to be one of them, even though she is technically a subordinate. Ellen's influence reaches far more broadly than her remit, and she is considered to be high potential within the top 200 of the organisation.

Words to practise courage

- 'When you do/say that, it makes me feel disappointed/ uncomfortable.'
- 'I understand what you are saying, and I have an alternative view to yours.'
- 'I'm not a fan of your comments/behaviour because they make me feel…'
- 'Personally, I'm not convinced that's the right course of action and I may have an alternative.'

Actions to practise courage

- Talk to a trusted colleague about your concerns and ask how they deal with the same problems.
- Role-play different situations with someone you trust and get their feedback.
- Brainstorm different scenarios that may require your courage, then script out some potential responses.

- Hold a safe space for your people and ask them for their honest views/opinions.
- Write your fears down in a journal and shine a light on them. Ask yourself what's the worst that can happen if they come true?

Behaviours to practise courage

- Are you getting outside of your comfort zone?
- Do you stand up for people, or just sympathise with them and moan about those causing the injustice?
- Do you call out any poor behaviour from your colleagues, or just gossip about them with others?
- Will you say what you truly want and make steps to get there, or sit and wish that someone will just offer it to you?
- Do you tell your boss when you don't agree with him or her, or just go along with everything they say?

Chapter 4

I AM STRONG

Peter was asked to lead a six-year-old, $100-million project in another department. His job was to review the health of the project, find efficiencies and ramp up delivery as soon as possible. He had a reputation for being a strong leader – fair and respectful – and he valued the skills and experience of his people, which meant his teams were engaged, empowered and productive.

The project was the brainchild of a long-term member of the executive team, and while it was initially a great idea, as the years passed the lack of progress started to hinder the objectives and things started to slip. There was a strong loyalty towards the executive who started the project, and Peter suspected this was blinding the objectivity of the executive team.

It didn't take long for Peter to realise that the project needed to end and he would need to influence everyone from the CEO down to also reach this conclusion.

This decision was going to be difficult for everyone to accept.

First, Peter earned the employees' trust. Without that he couldn't get anything done. They had fun, celebrated successes, reduced stress where possible and created bonds with each other. He then shifted his focus to his peers, including the executive who had created the project.

He met with each colleague to talk about the project's impact on their business. He introduced the idea of delivering through more efficient ways outside of the project, which would also reduce costs. They understood, but did Peter have a plan for the people impact?

Peter's final focus was the CEO who had a great deal of respect and gratitude for the executive who was the founder of the project. Peter had to tread carefully or risk more than he wanted to. He had to ensure the CEO and executive accepted the decision to close the project down.

Peter worked tirelessly to engage each function leader, stakeholder and employee to understand his decision. During the wind down of the project each one of the engineers was redeployed either inside or outside the company.

On the last day of the project, Peter met with the founding executive to have a final conversation about the project. The executive admitted that the project had gone on far longer than it should have, yet no one had 'had the balls' to close it, including himself.

He thanked Peter for having the strength to make the call, as well as for maintaining the dignity of all involved throughout the process.

Stand strong and steer

Not all situations that require your strength are as big as Peter's and worth millions of dollars. You will need to call on your strength for any number of situations, big and small.

You've got to have the guts to stand up, stand out and step in to whatever you are passionate about. All these actions require strength.

It isn't about the quality of the situation, it's about the ability to stay strong – usually in the face of criticism, backlash or upset you may cause. It's about drawing a line in the sand and backing yourself.

Strong leaders have the internal fortitude to make and stand by their decisions, to stand up for what they believe in, even if the odds are stacked against them.

This is where knowing and being clear on your purpose, or your 'why' will help you. If we look at Peter again, he was absolutely clear on why he was put into the role – to look for efficiencies and ramp up delivery. Team this with his purpose of valuing his people and he had clarity on the direction he was moving in.

But how do you find efficiencies and increase delivery as well as keep your people engaged, empowered and productive – and keep your stakeholders on board at the same time? It required Peter to make some tough calls and he knew that keeping his values and purpose front of mind would help him to guide his decision making, keeping him on course.

Gain trust

Peter first gained the trust of his people because he believed, based on experience, that when everyone felt valued they were more productive, empowered and engaged. An engaged workforce is more likely to trust and follow your decision making even if they don't like it.

He actively worked with his people to ensure they were ready to move elsewhere inside or outside the organisation. He developed trust with them so they were confident he had their best interests at heart, even though the decision he made would impact them immensely. He created an environment of support and safety, so his team were able to speak up, ask questions and voice their concerns.

Be inclusive

Peter then worked on his peers, keeping them informed and included in his thinking and decision making, all while working towards his goals of improved efficiency and delivery. He stood by his decisions with clear rationale, always referring back to why he was put into his job. He faced up to the difficult conversations with his peers and the founding executive, securing their help to support the redeployment of the engineers.

Manage up

Finally, Peter worked on his CEO, making sure he was across his thinking and working with him to achieve the best outcome for the company, stakeholders and people. He had to ensure that the CEO was supportive in managing the messages, conversations and decisions required.

Your purpose is like the rudder of a boat, without it you are travelling at the whim of outside forces, with no clear direction.

But why?

In their book *Leadership on the Line: Staying Alive through the Dangers of Leading*, Ron Heifetz and Marty Linsky talk about the importance of understanding your purpose, because when you are faced with tension, this will help you to accurately gauge the situation, so you can respond appropriately.

Your purpose also helps you to remain steady when you are faced with resistance. It keeps your ego in check and guides you when you are being swept up in the passion and emotions that usually accompany tough situations.

I recall working with a leader who needed to cut her staff numbers by half during a particularly poor period in the job market. Her clear purpose, which she had defined some years earlier, was 'to persist and inspire'. As she worked with each of her impacted employees over a number of months, she helped them to redeploy outside the organisation. Her persistence was inspiring to those around her. She remains in contact with most of them still.

Having strength and making the tough calls requires courage.

As we saw in the previous chapter, you can practise, build and strengthen your courage muscle, but it does mean accepting that sometimes you'll need to engage in conflict. By conflict I don't mean arguing or being difficult, I mean the type of conflict that is constructive, helps to get everyone's views and opinions out on the table, helps people to voice their concerns or displeasure, but all the while maintaining solid relationships with each other.

Showing strength can also mean sometimes being tough – making tough decisions, showing tough love, making tough calls and having tough conversations. All involve some level of conflict, and as a leader these are critical skills.

Conflict is part of life. If you try and avoid it, then it leads to things like a reduction in productivity, creativity and innovation – all essential ingredients in a healthy team and organisation.

In his book, *The Five Dysfunctions of a Team,* Patrick Lencioni talks about the importance of strong leadership teams being able to engage in conflict – constructively – to ensure that all views and opinions are tabled. He believes people are more willing to accept an outcome or decision they disagree with, if they have had the opportunity to fully have their voices heard.

As a leader the buck stops with you, so you must have the tough conversations to get your job done.

A catalyst for change

Have you ever been the recipient of a difficult conversation at some time in your career? It is usually remembered as a tough conversation that was hard to hear. You had to sit through some uncomfortable minutes listening to various home truths about what you were doing. It was tough to listen to and was probably equally as tough for the person delivering the message to you.

But how did you feel afterwards? Once you had got over the initial shock and disappointment of the message, did you find that you made changes, for better? Did you take the feedback on board and do something with it, and make changes in your life somehow? Perhaps you look back years later knowing that it was a defining moment in your career when your life changed.

In their book *The Power of Moments: Why Certain Experiences Have Extraordinary Impact*, Dan and Chip Heath talk about the requirement to create 'moments' in our lives and the lives of those around us. When we experience a moment of any kind, it is usually something that leaves a lasting impression on us, the memory stays with us, and can have either a good or bad impact on our lives. Sometimes it can even change us forever.

So if we think about this in reverse where you, as the leader, deliver a tough message to someone, think of yourself as the catalyst for change in that person's life.

This is an opportunity for you to be someone's turning point, to create a moment for them that they will never forget.

Respect versus fear

You've got to remember that delivery of this message, or talking tough, should never involve fear or you run the risk of developing a reputation as a bully. It's actually about earning respect and being respectful.

Neurologically, fear impedes your ability to engage in productive conversations because it influences the messages we hear. When we are in a state of fear our bodies produce cortisol, which impacts our ability to effectively interpret messages in conversations. This is when we become defensive and we are unable to empathise with others. Our ability to connect with anyone and understand their perspective becomes more difficult.

Respect and fear need to be reciprocal in an organisation. There needs to be respect shown for you and by you to those you work with, and low fear of you from others and from you to others, as shown in Figure 4.1.

Figure 4.1: Respect versus fear

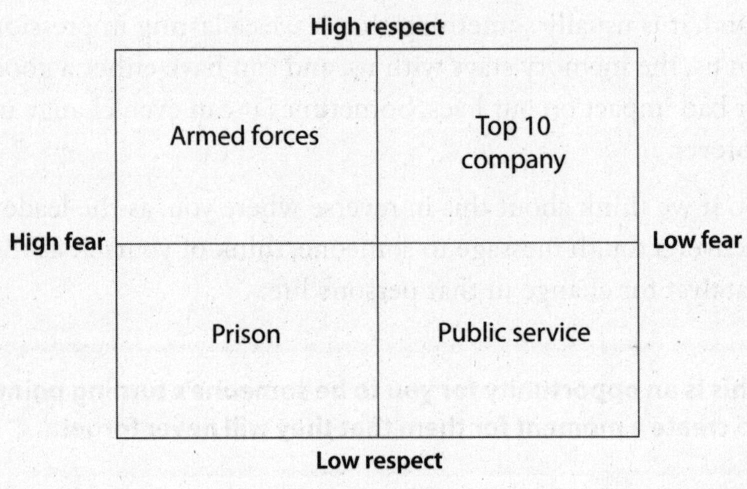

If you look at Figure 4.1, you can see some examples of the way particular industries operate, and where your fear and respect levels need to be if you are working in these organisations.

1. **Armed services** – are high in respect for authority and leadership, and they have a healthy dose of fear of consequences should anyone fall out of line.
2. **Prisons** – operate in a very high state of fear of violence and consequences and there is a very low respect for authority.
3. **Public service** – often you find low fear and low respect in this environment, resulting in a slow and bureaucratic work culture.
4. **Organisations** – (which sit in the top 10 organisations to work for) usually operate in a low fear (and high trust) environment and there's high respect for others within the organisation.

When you work in a culture of fear in an organisation, your ability to communicate and work productively is impacted significantly.

If respect and fear are at disproportionate levels you will create a very difficult work place.

Inside outside

When we are strong and can make difficult decisions, we often open ourselves up to ridicule, judgement and criticism. It goes with the territory of decision making. Those around you believe they have an obligation to provide you with their critique and feedback – solicited or not. This is where our internal strength needs to come into play.

While we are busy being strong on the outside, our insides are eating us alive with doubt and self-criticism and we start to second-guess our decisions.

In her book *The Power of Real Confidence – Learn How to Lead to Your Full Potential*, Michelle Sales highlights the impact of overthinking and negative self-talk as being two of the main culprits that destroy our confidence. Managing any self-talk to ensure it doesn't work counter to what you are trying to achieve is important. We've all worked with someone who over-compensates by being a tough nut on the outside and a marshmallow on the inside. This does nothing for their credibility.

Having confidence, both inside and outside, helps us to show others we are sure of what we are doing.

Set expectations

So how do we get stronger? How do we build up our strength to be able to draw on it when we need to, while also being respectful and courageous?

There are three ways to help you develop the skill of strength:

1. Set expectations with your team
2. Hold your people to account
3. Learn to say 'no'.

Let's look at each now.

1. Set expectations with your team

Spell it out for them. For example, 'I expect you to deliver X by the last day of the month' or 'My expectation is that you will complete this work by the end of the quarter.'

I know that sounds like overkill, and you may think surely people can think for themselves, but assuming is a dangerous exercise. At least if you spell it out for them, there is absolutely no room for misunderstandings, and if you need to have a difficult conversation later you can refer to these expectations. You also eliminate excuses such as 'I didn't know that', and you set the measurements for the minimum requirements of what you expect. Putting time into this up front will set you and your team up for success down the track.

2. Hold your people to account

Don't avoid a conversation or let it drag out too long hoping that things will fix themselves. The longer you leave it, hoping the situation will get better, the harder the conversation will be (and it will never get better!). Have the conversation, create the moment.

When people aren't held to account, then we create problems with performance management in organisations. Remember it's obvious to everyone when someone isn't performing and if you let it go, you damage more than your reputation as a strong leader.

3. Learn to say 'no' and stick with it

Be definitive with your 'no' and never be influenced to change your mind afterwards. Side conversations designed to create doubt and make you change your mind are an influencing tactic used by people who can't accept an outcome. Gather your data up front, make your decision and stand by your choice. If for some reason you find that your decision was the wrong one, own it, admit it and move forward.

Doing this sends two strong messages to everyone. The first is that you are human and sometimes you get it wrong; you are infallible, you make mistakes, but you don't dwell on them. You are continually reviewing assessing and moving forward. Secondly, it says that you learn from your mistakes and that your people should to.

Creating a learning environment by reducing the fear of failing is critical to business success and fosters a culture of innovation and creativity.

Remember, learning to say no takes practice. It's like learning to drive. When you first start out you are conscious of every gear change, pedal push and brake action. Eventually though driving becomes second nature to you. You can plan dinner, argue with your partner and drive all at the same time. When you do say no, remember to be firm but fair, give the benefit of the doubt, and keep reinforcing your decisions. Don't be worn down into saying yes. Like my kids, if they see a weakness they're in for the kill, so stay strong.

Power your performance

If you do these things the payoff will be enormous. You will gain respect for your decisions, regardless of whether your team agree with them or not, and they will follow through on your decisions. Performance will improve within your team because you have set your expectations, you are actively keeping them accountable and when performance slips, they know you will be onto it immediately.

Trust between you and your team members, your peers and your boss will increase because you are fair and stand by your decisions and values. They know they have your support and you know you have theirs.

Being tough is hard work, and like courage takes practice. It's not insurmountable though, and like all muscles the more you work at it the stronger it becomes.

Don't give up, if it doesn't work the first time, try again. Be strong!

Fair call

In 2016 I attended an Executive Leadership Workshop at Harvard on Leadership in the 21st Century. One of the participants was a young woman named Lina who, throughout the week would come and go during the lectures, often disrupting those around her. Lina was a source of distraction to some of the attendees who were annoyed at her disrupting their concentration during lectures, and so they complained about her to the lecturer and facilitators.

On the last day of the workshop, we were provided an open floor to give our feedback on the week, its highlights and lowlights and make comments. During this session Lina raised her hand and said that she had found the week to be insightful, beneficial and highly informative to the work she was doing. This was surprising to some of us given her noted lack of attendance.

The lecturer thanked her for her feedback and then commented on his surprise at her words, given that she was absent for much of the week. There was a silent collective intake of breath as his comments settled on the group.

The next hour of discussion was aimed firmly at the appropriateness of the lecturer and whether he should have called into question Lina's feedback in the manner that he did. Comments ranged from active support and commendation for calling the issue out, through to criticism and contempt for making Lina and other members of the group feel uncomfortable due to the exchange in dialogue.

Lina eventually provided the group with her heartfelt apology along with the reasons (completely plausible) as to why she needed to leave the room so often. With this context the group as a whole was accepting, compassionate and forgiving of her, however they seemed less forgiving of the lecturer.

The three takeaways for me were:

1. The strength required to withstand the criticism and backlash of being brave enough to call something out is significant and is required just as much as the strength needed for the action itself. To his credit, the lecturer remained firm and didn't apologise for his actions, and personally I don't believe he should have.
2. Just because you feel uncomfortable about witnessing an act of strength, it does not mean that the action is wrong. Your feelings of discomfort come from your own place and we need to be mature enough to recognise this.
3. Strength and courage are contagious. Be careful and mindful of your willingness to follow suit, this is how lynch mobs are created.

Strength and courage should always go hand-in-hand with dignity and respect. Never forget that!

Words to practise strength

- 'Thanks for your feedback, my decision remains unchanged.'
- 'I understand you may not agree, and my decision still stands.'
- 'What support do you need from me to help you to see my rationale?'

- 'This is what I believe in, and it has my full support.'
- 'This has my 100% support and backing.'

Actions to practise strength

- Give clear context on your decisions as this helps create clarity for those affected.
- Get comfortable with the need for conflict – it's a part of life, it's not easy, it's essential.
- Like courage, being tough takes practice. Don't give up if it doesn't work the first time.
- Own it, don't apologise for taking a stand or making a decision – it's yours to make.
- Stand clearly in your purpose. If you connect people to your purpose they may be more willing to take the risk because they can see where you are headed.

Behaviours to practise strength

- Are you prepared to make a call even if it's unpopular, or do you just sit on the fence?
- Do you have difficult conversations with your team, or just ignore things and hope it will get better (or they will leave!)?
- Do you keep your team accountable by calling them out, or let them get away with not performing or delivering?
- Do you ask each of your team members what they have been working on, or ask others what their colleagues are doing?
- How do you pose difficult questions to the person directly, so they can help build their strength too?

I AM A DIRECTIVE LEADER

I engineer the world around me

I move things around in my environment to get the best out of my people and the situation. This helps my people to step up and shine. I can see the system around me to get the most out of it for the good of the organisation.

I abdicate power to others

I can step back and out of things to give others a sense of ownership, to be empowered in their work. I don't sit back and relax while others do the work, instead I play my part, but I let others take the credit for the collective results of our efforts.

Chapter 5

I ENGINEER THE WORLD AROUND ME

Antanas Mockus was the Mayor of Bogota, Colombia, between 1995 and 2003. At this time, the city had a population of approximately 35 million, with about 120,000 kilometres of road and two million registered vehicles. In 1995 alone, motor vehicle injuries among males below the age of 35 was the second highest cause of death after violence. Corruption and street gangs were also on the rise, so Mockus knew he had a problem, a big one.

Mockus wasn't your average politician. Having resigned from his job at the Colombian National University where he was a mathematician and philosopher, he approached politics with a completely different view. Though he was seen by the population of Bogota as honest and trustworthy, thanks to his previous academic placement, he was also eccentric.

He once dressed up in a Superman costume and referred to himself as 'Supercitizen'.

So, in an effort to reduce the amount of fatalities resulting from traffic accidents, Mockus implemented an initiative that replaced corrupt traffic officers with mime artists. (Yes, really!)

His aim was twofold. Firstly, he wanted to reduce the number of corrupt traffic cops, and secondly he wanted to have the mime artists feign injury or offence when a motorist or pedestrian broke the road rules. He effectively created acceptance or non-acceptance from the public of those who were breaking the rules. This is also known as the court of public opinion.

The result? People began to change their behaviour. Road rules were obeyed, pedestrians were given right of way, and traffic light signals were observed. In his first term of office, Mockus successfully reduced the rate of traffic fatalities by more than 50%. He also removed the 1,800 corrupt traffic officers, replacing them with the national police service. Mockus earned the trust of the people of Bogota, so much so that he also went on to increase taxes by convincing citizens to voluntarily pay additional tax.

This is engineering at its best – manoeuvring situations, circumstances or the physical work environment to get the best outcome for all involved.

Change the outcome

Early in my career I was asked if I would like to present to a group of senior managers on the success we were having with selling a particular product. I was terrified and because I had the choice I graciously declined. I prepared all the notes and the visuals for my boss to present but I was scared of doing it myself in case I made a goose of myself.

On the day of the presentation, my leader called me and said he was caught up in another meeting and couldn't attend, so I needed to step in to do it. He assured me that I had all the information and I was the only person who could present it. I didn't have much choice, so I went in and presented the information. It went really well and afterwards I told my boss proudly about the presentation. He then confessed to me that he was sitting in an office downstairs doing some of his work and that he had set the whole thing up. After recovering from the shock, I was grateful to him. It worked in helping me to get over my fear of presenting, particularly when the work was mine to begin with.

This is a great example of how you can engineer a situation to put others first to get a positive outcome for your team, your peers or your boss.

As a result, your people and peers will learn that you are supportive of their development, you are not there solely for the sake of your own career and you are definitely a team player.

Your boss will see you as more collaborative, and overall you will show that you are leading through your actions, building better connections with those you work with and in turn you end up having a positive influence on everyone around you.

This helps to create a positive work environment and culture.

Get physical

At work, engineering situations might involve physically altering the environment through your words, actions and behaviour.

You might:

- **Change the surroundings – Take your boss on a walk-n-talk away from the office.** By simply moving the environment away from your boss's office you may get a different outcome. When we walk alongside more senior people we subconsciously reduce hierarchy, making it easier to speak up and influence.
- **Change the channel – Work with your leader's personal assistant to get things done.** I once worked with a leader, Sam, who asked his boss to ring some of his team to congratulate them on the work they were doing. His boss kept getting side-tracked and couldn't seem to make it happen, so Sam went direct to his boss's PA to schedule time in his diary specifically to make the calls. His boss made the calls – much to the delight of the recipients.
- **Change your language – Use words that you want to hear.** For example, if you want people to be more conscious of the customer, use the term customer in

every conversation you have. Language and behaviour are contagious, you only need to look at any culture to see how powerful they are.

Manipulating the situation or environment (as shown in the examples above), relies on your intention and your transparency, as shown in Figure 5.1.

Figure 5.1: Intention versus transparency

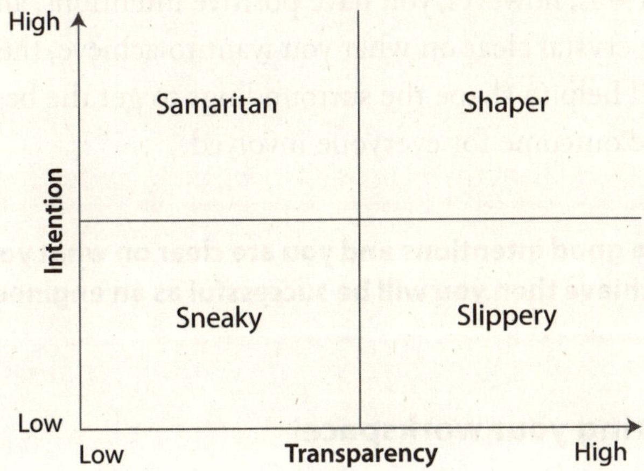

Looking at the figure, you can see that there are four types of behaviour that are influenced by your intention and your transparency:

1. **Sneaky** – If your intention is negative and your transparency is low, then it isn't clear why you are doing what you are doing, and you are not intent on getting a positive outcome for anyone other than yourself.

2. **Slippery** – If you are clear on what you are trying to achieve, but it's only for your own good, then you can appear to be a slippery salesperson, or narcissistic.
3. **Samaritan** – If your intentions are positive, yet you're unclear or it isn't evident why you are doing what you are doing, you may come across as always doing good for people but no-one's sure why.
4. **Shaper** – If, however, you have positive intentions, and you are crystal clear on what you want to achieve, then you will help to shape the surroundings to get the best possible outcome for everyone involved.

If you have good intentions and you are clear on what you want to achieve then you will be successful as an engineer.

Engineering your workspace

There are many examples of engineered environmental changes that occur in society that induce change to the way we behave. The iPhone is a classic.

Since its introduction, we have been able to work from anywhere in the world. We take photos of our food. We are able to go into complete strangers' lives and see what they are doing, eating and wearing.

Another example of environmental engineering and the impact it has on behaviour is supermarkets positioning milk at the furthest back corner of the store. This makes sure you walk past numerous products on the way to get your milk and back, the hope being to tempt you to buy more items.

Another one dieters will be familiar with is the concept of 'shrinking your plate' to make it seem as if you are eating the same amount of food, when in fact you are eating less because it fills a smaller plate.

A way that engineering can play out at work is by changing the work floor plan.

One organisation I worked with supplied a small table and chairs off to the side of a desk in their senior leader's offices. The aim here was to provide an additional space where conversations could be held. When employees enter the office to speak to a leader, the leader can often remain distracted by their email and messages on their computer. By providing an additional space, the leader and employee can move away from the desk and sit and have an uninterrupted conversation without distraction.

Workplaces are becoming more and more open plan with breakout areas, alcoves, small or standing tables, all designed to change the way we work by taking us out of offices and creating spaces to be more collaborative.

How different is your current work environment to the way you worked 10 years ago?

I have a coaching client who, when she needs to spend time focusing on strategic issues, will block her diary out for two hours, move to a small meeting room and turn her mobile phone off. In so doing, she is changing her environment to enable her to have the space to focus on what she needs to.

The balcony or the dance floor?

The best way to start to find opportunities to engineer situations is to look around you and be aware of what is going on. Be curious about situations. Ask yourself what are some of the external factors that are impacting a situation, which if tweaked could change things or provide more opportunity?

One technique developed by Ron Heifetz, Alexander Grashow and Marty Linsky from Harvard University is an adaptive leadership process of Observe, Interpret and Intervene.

1. Observe

When you observe a situation that you would like to influence you need to have both a higher level view and a lower level view. Heifetz et al use the terms Balcony View (high level) and Dance Floor View (low level) because each provides distinctly different information.

When you are on a dance floor, you see the people who are around you, within a few metres. When you stand on the balcony, however, and look down at the dancers you see the individuals within the system, you see different groups of people, and you see different types of dance styles, all providing you with a greater perspective and a broader understanding. So, using both perspectives will provide you with more data when assessing a situation.

You need to be both on the balcony and the dance floor at different times.

Use the dance floor view to get the details of the situation and use the balcony to get better perspective and view the overall system in which the situation is taking place. Nothing ever happens in isolation and your balcony view will provide you with context.

2. Interpret

In the movie *Vantage Point*, there is an attempted assassination of the US President at a political event. In the movie, the same story is told several times from the perspective of several different characters. Each one sees the event in a different way, which ultimately poses the question of what truth actually is.

Understanding the situation from different points of view can help you to make an informed interpretation of it and decide upon the potential actions you can use in your intervention.

To fully interpret a situation ask yourself "What's going on here?", "Who are the primary players?" and "What are they trying to achieve?". By understanding what's happening from different perspectives you can make a much more informed decision about what you can do, your intervention or actions.

3. Intervene

Once you have observed and interpreted a situation, try to develop a hypothesis that will inform what intervention or actions you can take.

Always develop a plan and a backup plan. If the first plan doesn't work, recognise it and admit it to yourself and move on to the next one. Being able to adapt is key in your intervention. You can look at these steps as mini experiments to prove or disprove your hypothesis.

You should use resources in your interventions that are available to you and within your control. They're not trying to solve world peace!

Your intervention will depend on your hypothesis, but my advice is to keep things simple. If you start to overcomplicate or change too much it's going to get messy.

Interventions can be as simple as changing furniture in an office to shift a dynamic, asking a peer to mentor one of your direct reports, or taking your boss out for a walking meeting to get her to buy into your new idea. In all instances, doing something is better than doing nothing.

The process of Observe, Interpret, Intervene is designed to be iterative, so use it in an ongoing way, re-tweaking as you go.

By using the process of observing, interpreting and intervening you are able to view things from different perspectives, interpret situations in different ways and provide viable alternatives to achieve what you need to.

By opening your eyes, expanding your consciousness to what's going on around you and thinking differently about how you change or influence, you will be able to adapt your environment to suit. Be creative in your interventions and always have a back-up plan or two, in case the first one doesn't work!

What's your currency?

In their book *Influence without Authority*, Cohen and Bradford talk about the value of identifying someone's currency. By currency they mean identifying what is valuable to a person that can be traded or exchanged with something you have, to get a desired outcome.

This is all based on the law of reciprocity – if you do something for someone they usually want to return the favour.

By understanding more about the people you work with, you will be able to determine quite quickly what their currency is, and be able to identify opportunities to offer this currency for things in return.

You could include these currencies when determining your interventions through the Observe, Interpret, Intervene process. For example, say one of your colleagues values recognition and wants to look good in front of the boss, if you give up some of the recognition for work you have done together, it may help the next time you need that colleague to return the favour.

By understanding currencies you are also able to influence those around you, becoming more effective and productive in your own role, leading to the broader function or organisation achieving their goals.

Everyone values something, it is really a matter of observing those you know to help you to figure out what they value. Once you do understand them more you can determine what you have, or where you can get it, to offer a trade – authentically, of course! This is not about using people's currency against them or holding them to ransom.

It's about making connections between what you need and what others need, and making it work together.

Focused freedom

By shifting the environment, you become better able to influence more broadly through gaining a greater understanding of different perspectives. You are able to influence your boss, peers and people because you understand the environment they operate in, you can observe, interpret and take actions to get the best outcome for everyone involved. You understand people's currencies and are able to offer and ask for the things you need to get the job done.

You start to put your people in situations that will help them to stretch and shine. This will increase their loyalty and respect for you and develop their own leadership capability. When they start to develop and become more confident, they are then able to manage more than their own roles and become more influential in their own right. As their confidence grows, trust builds, which in turn allows you more freedom to focus on the right things at the right time.

What your environment says about you

I was once asked to work with a leadership team to help them to work better together and develop their strategy for the next three years. We agreed an off-site would help them to achieve these two goals.

During the offsite I observed that one of the team members, Gerard was quite disengaged throughout the day. He would sit looking out the window, deep in thought, not participating in the work we were discussing. I tried to bring him into the conversation multiple times. He would nod, make a one-line comment and then go back to his apparent day-dreaming.

During one of the breaks I asked the leader if this was standard behaviour for Gerard. He acknowledged that this was indeed the case, and that he had raised it with him previously, without much improvement.

During the next session of the day, I observed the group dynamics to determine if there was anything happening among the group. Nothing was apparent, until I took the opportunity to mention to Gerard that he seemed distracted and was there something I could help him with to get him re-engaged. This seemed to surprise him, as though he wasn't aware he was dis-engaged. I continued to observe both Gerard and the group for the remainder of the day.

In my post off-site review, I asked the leader if I could attend one of the team's weekly meetings. This would enable me to get another perspective, this time from the dance floor.

At the meeting, the group were speaking over each other to the point of yelling, cutting each other off mid-conversation and the dialogue was going around in circles not getting to an outcome or decision. All the while Gerard mostly remained silent.

It's no wonder Gerard behaved the way he did, he had probably given up trying to compete with his colleagues for air time. I now had a different perspective and was able to determine some alternative interventions. I decided to tweak their environment.

I scheduled a session with the team to teach them a number of techniques based on effective dialogue and Conversational Intelligence. I showed them how to listen to hear not respond, and then how to make sure they really understood what was being said. I got them to use a simple, yet effective, tool called a talking stick (aka a Biro) which gave everyone equal talking and listening time.

The result was positive, particularly for Gerard. He now had the space to speak and to be heard, as did his colleagues, without the need to fight for space. Using the observation, interpretation and intervention process provided some simple yet effective changes to the environment and it helped Gerard and his team to move forward.

Words to practise engineering

- 'What's actually happening here?'
- 'What can we do to get the best possible outcome for everyone?'
- 'What can we leverage to tweak the environment?'
- 'How can we change things around to get a good outcome?'

- 'If you were my mentor/boss/colleague what would your advice be?' then 'if you were my friend, would your advice be different?' (You're changing their status by asking them to respond from different positions i.e. mentor, friend, colleague, coach.)
- 'You take the credit this time.' (That one might hurt a little!)

Actions to practise engineering

- Identify work outside of your function that you can get your direct reports involved in so that they develop a specific skill.
- Ask a colleague to invite one of your direct reports to work on something outside their current job to get some additional experience or exposure.
- Practise observation, interpretation and intervention the next time you identify an issue.
- Observe your colleagues and think about their currency. Do you have anything to exchange?
- Be curious about what is going on around you.

Behaviours to practise engineering

- Do you look for ways to make your people look good, or mainly for yourself to look good?
- Are you working feverishly in the background or always out in front in the spotlight?
- Do you naturally connect people with mutual benefits or are you puzzled by why someone would do this?

- Do you spend most of your time with your people, on the floor or in their environment, or are you in your office with the door closed?
- How much time do you spend with your colleagues, boss and people outside your immediate work space to understand what they do and what their challenges are? Do you know they even have challenges?

Chapter 6

I ABDICATE POWER TO OTHERS

Dee prided herself on being a great leader. What she said she would deliver, always got delivered. What she said she would do, always got done. She saw this as one of her strengths.

Yet it wasn't without its hard work and constant management. Dee found over the years that she couldn't solely depend on others to do their job and come through with the goods. No, that would sometimes leave her exposed to risk, which she didn't like.

Dee felt that to make sure she was going to get the job done, she needed to be across the work that her people were doing. The detail and timing were critical. If she was responsible for it, then she needed to be all over it. This would make sure that delivery was on time, within budget and her stakeholders were happy.

This meant she was tired and stressed, but it was the price she happily paid for maintaining her reputation. And without her reputation, she felt she had nothing.

Sure, her people weren't overly happy working at her company. She had noticed that the engagement scores of her team had reduced for the third year in a row. The feedback from her team was that they didn't think they were learning anything, or that their ideas weren't being listened to. They also believed that they didn't have any ownership of the deliverables, and that they weren't trusted.

Well, they got that part right! Time and again Dee had been let down by people who hadn't come through on time, or were significantly over budget. She then had to go and explain this to her boss and she didn't particularly like that because it inferred that she wasn't in control of what was going on.

No wonder she was so stressed! She was always answering, directing and facilitating outcomes. It was like she was doing everyone's job as well as her own.

Do you recognise Dee? Is there someone like Dee in your workplace? Or is this person perhaps you?

Dee didn't know how to let go and abdicate responsibility to her team to have more control, influence and ownership.

Accept the way the cat is skinned

As a leader you need to let your people step up into their roles and make an active contribution by stepping back and letting them own them. This is often harder than you think!

When you are abdicating responsibility to someone else it can feel as if you are giving up complete control. Let me be clear, though, abdicating does not mean a complete *lack* of ownership on your part. As the leader you must retain overall ownership and back your people when you need to.

Abdicating power is letting go enough that you are comfortable with the outcome, even though you may not have reached the outcome in the same way.

As the saying goes, 'there are more ways to skin a cat' and you need to accept the way the cat is skinned. Make no mistake, this will be uncomfortable for you at first because you're giving up a certain amount of control over the situation. That's hard.

When your team come to you all the time for the answers to their problems and expect you to provide solutions, this says to your brain "I have value". You feel as though you are actively contributing to getting things done. Hell, you're the boss, isn't that why you are here, to solve all the problems?

Like most things, though, enjoying too much of something becomes a weakness and you run the risk of getting addicted to having all the answers for everyone. Genetically we are all wired to want to feel valued as this is one of the contributing factors to our self-esteem and self-worth. But if it happens too much we become absorbed by how it makes us feel.

When you provide your people with the solution to their problems you get a shot of oxytocin and dopamine making you feel really great. You feel important, you feel needed, you're in control.

On the reverse of this, when you micromanage your employees you are taking away their ability to control their own work.

This in turn takes away their certainty in the way they are able to manage their environment. To their brains, when you threaten their certainty this causes stress, making them less likely to be engaged, innovative and collaborative, and you will lose their respect and possibly increase their fear.

Credit in and credit out

We have all seen or worked with someone who has taken abdicating their responsibility to heart and developed it into a work ethic. This is the person who sits in a job, taking up the position, doing little, delegating everything and accepting responsibility for nothing.

Managing how much you delegate and how you empower others takes a conscious effort to make sure that you don't end up doing nothing.

Abdicating power to others should always be to the benefit of your people, your function and your organisation, for good and not evil.

It also depends on who you are dealing with to determine how to do it.

Your boss

When you are managing your boss, you sometimes need to relinquish:

- **the battle to win the war.**
  Whether your boss is right or wrong, you sometimes need to let it go and accept that it is so.
- **the credit for the work you have done.**
  After all, making your boss look good will usually work in your favour somewhere down the line. It's like building a line of credit for future use.
- **your good ideas.**
  Sometimes, no matter how you present a good idea, some bosses just don't get it or the timing isn't quite right. Recognise when you are not getting anywhere and move on.
- **your view of success.**
  When your boss has a different view of what success looks like, sometimes you need to work to her agenda.

Your peers

When it comes to your peers you may need to move away from:

- **taking the credit (again) for work you have done and this may work in your favour.**
  Be mindful of never absolving yourself from responsibility to the extent that it means your peers

will be required to take the fall for something – this is not what empowering is about.

- **taking the higher ground.**
  You don't always need to be better than those you work with and they may at times be smarter than you. Appreciating their skills, experience and ideas goes a long way to building rapport and trust with your colleagues.
- **going it alone.**
  Actively and genuinely collaborating with your peers sends a strong message upwards and downwards throughout your organisation.

Your team

When you empower the people you lead, you can:

- **let them fail safely.**
  Stepping back and supporting them when they fail is a great way for them to learn. Always ensure that you have a thorough debrief of the situation to help them understand clearly what went wrong and what they could do differently next time. This self-reflection creates new neural pathways in the brain and, with the addition of a coaching conversation to debrief, you create a much higher chance of the employee learning from it.
- **not have the solution for everything.**
  This is a great way to empower your people. This means being comfortable to accept that the solution they arrive at for a problem, even though it may not have been what

you would have done or what you have tried in the past. Sometimes a solution sounds the same as something done before, however, different minds and perspectives in play will change the subtle nuances of the past play, therefore enabling a different outcome.

- **Give up the credit (again – there's a theme here!).** Stepping back and letting your people shine and be rewarded for their hard work is a great way to show them humility, build their trust in you and reward them. When you simply thank an employee for their work you access the same mental areas of the brain that light up when a person has a financial reward. This has a very powerful impact on us mentally and it's the easiest thing for a leader to do.

What you are trying to create by abdicating some of your power and responsibility is a culture of empowered people.

When you step back from situations you help people to share in the leadership of the function as well as accept accountability both for their mistakes and their successes. By not solving their problems for them, they also learn to think for themselves and develop their own leadership style. Your ability to create change more effectively grows, while their control over their environment increases, reducing stress and improving engagement.

Abdication also gives you the ability to create capacity in your work life and reduce your own stress. When you create capacity, you find that you have more time to focus on additional activities like increasing your networks across the organisation, creating more time to focus on strategic issues, planning and building relationships within and outside of your team, which in turn leads to greater influence up and beyond your remit.

Put it into practice

So, what does abdication look like in practice? How can you put this technique into action?

There are three techniques you could practise:

1. Hand it over
2. Ask questions
3. Be silent.

Let's explore each.

1. Hand it over

The next time you have a problem to solve, hand it over to your team to discuss and debate and offer solutions. Here's the hard part: while they are doing this sit quietly, listen and observe.

Resist the temptation to enter the discussion or debate. This will be hard for you because our minds are constantly reviewing, assessing and developing answers and solutions to the things we see and hear. It will take a conscious effort not to get involved, but it will be worth it.

By observing and listening you will hear potential solutions that you may not have considered, enabling the creativity and innovation of your people. You are also increasing the level of control and insight experienced by everyone, which is proven to increase wellbeing and positivity.

You may observe the dynamics at play within your team. Who contributes and who doesn't, how accepting are they of each other's ideas, how do they interact with each other?

2. Ask questions

A great technique developed by Judith Glaser in her book *Conversational Intelligence: How great leaders build trust and get extraordinary results*, is asking questions that you don't know the answer to. This is a good way to find out what people think about issues and how you can potentially tackle things differently.

You would use language like:

- "What do you think about it?"
- "How would you handle it?"
- "What are your suggestions on how to manage this?".

These are all questions that involve someone providing you with their thoughts and suggestions that you couldn't possibly know without asking them. The key here is to ensure that you listen to what they are saying, and don't discount or discredit their suggestions. Keep an open mind and a closed mouth.

3. Be silent

All too often people will say something – anything – to fill the gap made by silence. We just can't stand waiting with our own thoughts.

I often stay silent when I facilitate meetings or discussions because of exactly that reason. When I use this technique, someone will always speak to fill the void. This is a great way to ensure that people do speak and are heard.

Practise being OK with some of the solutions that are suggested by other people. Just because it's not what you would do, doesn't mean that it's either not going to work or is simply the wrong solution. This is a great opportunity to help your people feel trusted, supported and empowered, particularly if what they suggest doesn't work. Always debrief the outcome afterwards, good or bad, and ask a question you don't know the answer to, for example, "What are your insights from how this played out?".

Using abdication in managing the relationships that you have in your workplace sets a good example to those around you.

Increasing innovation

When you take a step back from providing all the solutions, you enable those around you to step up and into their own leadership style. You are saying that you are open and accepting of their ideas and solutions, that you don't have all the answers to all the problems, and it's OK to sometimes get things wrong as long as you learn from them.

As your team start to see that the solutions they are offering are listened to and sometimes accepted, they themselves begin to become more courageous in what they offer. This then leads to increased innovation and creativity in problem solving.

It also means less stress for you in having to provide all the answers all the time.

Remember Dee from the beginning of the chapter? Her people were unhappy, and so was he. She was stressed, overworked and in serious threat of burnout. Her people felt disempowered, not trusted, unhappy and not listened to. Her engagement scores were on a downward slide year on year – all because she wasn't prepared to abdicate some responsibility to those around her. She wasn't even prepared to try.

The aim of abdication is as much about you stepping back as it is about you enabling people to step in. It's about relinquishing some of your need for control and handing that over to someone else.

As a result, you'll help create a culture of shared responsibility, openness to new ideas and solutions, increased collaboration across functions and an increase in trusted relationships.

It's within your control to let go of control.

Just try it and see.

Step back to step up

Maria led a team of five managers who were not working together. This was a constant source of frustration for Maria, as she could see the potential in each one, and if combined it was clear they could achieve some amazing things. Maria was having trouble helping them to realise that they weren't working together. They thought they were.

Maria had to go to a conference for a week in October and asked the team to focus on maintaining the overall level of faults for the whole function so that customers were not impacted any further while she was away. This would require the team to work together to ensure that an appropriate solution was developed and implemented. She didn't think it was too hard an issue for them to solve, they just had to talk to each other. She also decided that she wouldn't get anyone to fill her role while she was away, preferring to let the team step up into their own leadership.

On her return Maria was disappointed and frustrated. The team had only focused on their own patch, which resulted in the issue not being solved and even more customers being impacted. She had to get them to see that they had to change.

Maria met with each leader individually to talk about the issue. She shared her disappointment and frustration and how she now felt that she couldn't trust them. She asked them how they could have handled the situation better. What actions could they have taken in hindsight that may have helped the situation?

During the conversation, each expressed their own remorse at having let her down and could see how their behaviour was disappointing. She then spoke to them as a group, reinforcing her disappointment and that she could see the potential in the team to really step up and into being great leaders, together.

Over the next few months, Maria continued to try to get the team to work together, always reinforcing her messages of collaboration and getting them more involved with the decision making. She started to back away from the day-to-day management of the function, seeking her leaders' input and backing the decisions they were making – even though at times she was genuinely concerned that they wouldn't work. Some of them failed, but Maria was quick to offer her support and help them to learn from the situation ensuring they knew she was there to back them.

Then came a restructure, and Maria knew this was going to be a test for the team. She brought them all together and asked them to lead the work across the function, letting them know she would be there if they needed her, but essentially, they would be leading the work themselves.

She asked them to come up with the solution for the function, and to present it to her as a stakeholder, not their leader. They worked hard together and came up with a great solution that they presented to Maria. They had met their required cost reduction and the people targets allocated to them, and Maria could tell they were proud of the work they had done. In the end they delivered what they needed to in a collaborative and engaging way. The test would be the engagement scores for the function.

They were all pleasantly surprised to see engagement had risen by 5% even though there was significant change experienced by the teams. By stepping back, Maria was able to help her team to step into their own leadership roles for the function, and achieve a great outcome, together.

Words to practise abdication

- 'How would you go about solving this problem?'
- 'What do you think we should do here?'
- 'You have my 100% support and backing.'
- 'I've also learned something here.'
- 'How could we learn together from this situation?'
- 'I understand what you are going through, it's not the end of the world.'
- 'Is there a silver lining here for us?'

Actions to practise abdication

- Step back and out of the way to let your people get on with it.
- Stay silent, don't offer solutions or opinions to fix a problem.
- Let others find their voices.
- Listen actively to what your people are saying.
- Avoid judging people when they offer alternatives to yours.
- Accept other ideas even though you are sceptical.
- Let your people fail safely rather than stepping in and saving the day.
- Accept you are not the hero.

Behaviours to practise abdication

- Are you comfortable stepping away and letting your people stand out, or are you always after the limelight?
- When was the last time one of your people failed and you comforted and supported them?
- How often do you accept the input from others and use their ideas?
- Are you constantly annoyed that your leader doesn't give you credit for the work you have done?
- Are you always fighting battles with your boss, your peers or your people?
- Do you always feel as though you need to have the answer?
- Do you need to be in control or across everything that is going on in your function?

I AM A PERCEPTIVE LEADER

I trust and am trusted

I am trusted by those who rely on me and I trust those who I need to. I know that trust is an ongoing process, not an event, and that I should never take advantage of trust. I understand that it takes time to build trust, yet it can be destroyed in an instant. I know that trust should be nurtured and cared for with seriousness and sensitivity and above all never taken for granted. I know that trust is at the heart of every relationship I have.

I can be vulnerable

I see vulnerability as a strength, not a weakness and I know it means opening up to those around me by being able to say that I'm unsure or may not know something. It also means sometimes I have to let go of control when I need to. I understand the business world is a tough environment with deeply entrenched challenges making it hard to be vulnerable. I will need to draw on my strength and courage to be vulnerable.

Chapter 7

I TRUST AND AM TRUSTED

Jim has worked at the same organisation for a number of years. He usually comes in on the early train and is at his desk by 7.30am having picked up his morning coffee on the way in. He wears his name-tag proudly along with his 230,000 co-workers across the world.

Jim has a desk in head office and he sits next to Tony who is an executive in the company. Tony lives with his wife Sandy and their two kids Chip aged 12 and Maddie 9. When Jim arrives each morning, he is often greeted by Tony along with many other employees on the shop floor and they usually have friendly banter as Jim makes his way through to his desk.

Like those he works with, Jim's employment contract is a one-page document and includes a clause that says if he doesn't do his work he can get fired. He believes that if he is happy at work and is treated well by his employer this then flows on to how employees treat their customers. During his career Jim has seen this play out many times and it's now part of his leadership philosophy.

He has spent a lot of time understanding and working with the people around him at all levels and he really believes in the values of the organisation. The company gives him and all its employees health insurance, which isn't common within the US retail industry, and it's one of the reasons employee turnover is so low here. He also believes that in business 'you have to take the shit with the sugar' when dealing with success.

During the financial crisis, when many retailers in the US were cutting jobs, closing stores and some were going out of business, the company refused to sack anyone and maintained employees' health benefits. Customers continued to pay their membership fees and price increases were limited to no more than 14%. The company values honesty and respect from all their suppliers and once pulled a well-known brand of soft drink from their shelves because they weren't receiving the lowest possible price from them.

While Jim isn't paid much compared to his counterparts in other similar sized organisations across the US, he's quite happy with what he gets.

When I first read about Jim, I inherently knew he was a trustworthy guy. I knew this because he knows about the person and family of the guy sitting next to him. He believes in treating employees well. He connects with the values of the company he works for. And he believes in fairness in pay, regardless of where you sit in the organisation. I'm sure you agree.

Now, can you guess who Jim is?

I'll give you a clue. He is the founder and CEO of one of the largest worldwide brands …

…Costco.

Yep, Jim Sinegal doesn't believe he should be paid any more than the $350k he receives, even though his brand is valued at approximately US$18 billion. Costco has about 90 million members who purchase every week from a range of groceries, appliances, baked goods, electronics, apparel, books and a number of other services. Jim retired in 2011 having left a significant legacy in Costco and he now serves on the board as a company adviser and director.

As business tycoon Warren Buffett once said: 'Trust is like the air we breathe. When it's present, nobody really notices. But when it's absent, everybody notices.'

Trust me

At the heart of any personal and professional relationship is trust. It has to be, otherwise work wouldn't get done, people wouldn't turn up and customers wouldn't buy from us.

When you have relationships based on trust you are more likely to do more, be more and get more in return.

In his article 'How to Build Trust in an Organization' Chris Hitch Ph.D., Program Director of UNC Executive Development says: "Trust is earned through action and interaction. Action gives people evidence while interaction shows openness to others' needs and ideas."

Hitch goes on to explain that trust comprises three core components:

1. Credibility
2. Respect
3. Fairness.

When you think about Jim from Costco, he showed his credibility through being open and accessible to all his people – no matter who they were or where they came from in the organisation, he had a fold-out chair for them. He has no airs and graces like other CEOs and saw himself as one of the team. He showed respect by treating employees well, providing them with healthcare and he had a philosophy of looking after employees first and foremost. He showed fairness by not being over paid, answering his own phone, having no office and buying his own coffee.

It's no wonder that Costco had the lowest employee turnover in the retail industry as well as the company's highest annual profit in the two years leading up to his retirement in 2011.

As a leader, it is imperative to learn the language of trust and to work hard at ensuring that trust is at the heart of the relationships that you manage. Your leader needs to trust you to get the job done, and you must be able to trust that he or she has your back when you need them.

The ability for you to be able to speak your mind openly and honestly, always with respect and without fear of damaging your relationship, is a good sign of healthy trust.

There must also be mutual trust between you and your peers to ensure that you can have conversations that include robust debate without fear of redress or reprisal.

Being able to trust the people who work for you to get their job done, to ensure that they know you have their back when they need you and that they will be listened to, engaged with, respected and treated fairly creates empowered employees which increases engagement and retention.

A study completed by Paul Zak (author of *The Neuroscience of Trust*) found that in comparison with organisations where there is low trust, companies with high trust report:

- 74% less stress
- 106% more energy at work
- 50% higher productivity
- 13% less sick days
- 76% more engagement
- 29% more satisfaction with their lives
- 40% less burnout with employees.

Having a work environment that fosters open and honest dialogue between employees will lead to higher creativity and innovation and a reduction in fear and stress.

Top five trust killers

Throughout my career, I have worked with many leadership teams and seen how low trust can impact the overall performance, development and culture of a function.

Here are my top five killers of trust that you need to look out for:

1. **Inaction** – leaders are often reluctant to take action, particularly in times of uncertainty. For example, they refuse to appoint someone to a more senior role because they believe that the person doesn't have enough of the right experience in one aspect of the role. They would rather not appoint anyone than trust that the person will step up and into the promotion and do a really good job at it.

2. **Competition** – too much competition between employees when it comes to achieving targets and key performance indicators does nothing to foster an environment of trust. I believe that employees need to be motivated, however, I don't believe that individual targets are conducive to creating a trusting culture within organisations.

3. **Fear** – people live in a constant state of fear due to perceived threats such as organisational restructures,

poorly managed change and merger/acquisitions. When we are under constant threat and information is scarce, trust decreases rapidly.

4. **Blame** – at the first sign of trouble, fingers point in all directions trying to deflect blame onto others. Some organisations resemble bus depots because so many people are thrown under them!
5. **Gossip** – when people are talking about each other or about their leaders, trust is always absent. When teams have a high level of trust and respect for each other, gossiping and back-biting are either shut down, or never happen in the first place.

On the flip side, trust can be restored with time, effort and focus. Most importantly, a culture of trust starts at the top and will filter down throughout the organisation at all levels.

Start by focusing on others first, increasing collaboration and communication and building transparency into as much as you can.

Remember, building trust is a journey, not an event.

Disconnect to connect

As we discussed earlier, as humans we create families, build tribes and come together as communities. It's fundamentally how we have survived as a species for so long.

We create these connections primarily through the conversations that we have with each other and the behaviours that we show others. Yet we live in a time when we are so distracted by electronics, social media and emails that we are losing the ability to connect.

A study published in the *American Journal of Preventative Medicine* surveyed 7,000 people aged between 19 and 32 and found that those who spent the most time on social media had double the chance of experiencing social isolation through a low sense of social belonging and fewer experiences with fulfilling relationships.

You only need to poke your head up from your phone on the train one morning and have a look around. See anyone having a conversation? I once worked with a guy who would say good morning to his team via instant messenger. They all sat within a 10-metre radius of him.

If we can't connect with each other through conversations, how can we expect to trust each other?

If we can't build trust, how can we expect to be empowered and to empower our people to work effectively with anyone else and to build teams and communities?

We lose billions of dollars each year on low productivity, profits and shareholder returns as a result of our lack of trust in organisations (Covey, 2016).

Additionally, a study completed by Brown, Gray, McHardy and Taylor in 2014, found a positive relationship between trust in the workplace and financial performance, labour productivity and product or service quality in organisations.

These are reasons enough to ensure that developing and maintaining trust is a priority in our everyday lives.

It is critical that we establish and maintain trust in our relationships, teams and organisations to ensure sustainability, longevity and financial success.

Laying a firm foundation

How then do we build and maintain trust in the relationships that we manage?

There are five areas to focus on to build and maintain trust – no matter if you're managing your team, your colleagues, your clients or your boss:

1. Walk your talk
2. Be present
3. Listen to understand
4. Share common ground
5. Be vulnerable.

Let's explore each.

1. Walk your talk

One of the most common complaints that I hear in organisations is that their leaders say one thing and do another.

As an example, I once worked in an organisation where the CEO always touted the importance of talking to employees at all levels, to understand and listen to their ideas and thoughts. Yet on any given day he would catch the goods lift up to his floor, seemingly to avoid the normal lifts and getting caught in conversation with any of the employees. Needless to say, his credibility slipped when people heard about this.

Ensuring that you do what you say you will do and are consistent in your words and actions speaks volumes in organisations.

As a leader you are constantly on show, being watched by those around you. Subconsciously we are always observing what people say and do. Being aware of this and behaving in the correct way in response to this helps us build credibility and respect from those around us.

2. Be present

When you have a conversation with a person and you are not fully present, you are causing damage to your relationship with that person. Here's why.

When we are talking to someone and they are not doing things like looking us in the eyes, nodding in agreement or showing signs that they understand what we are saying, we experience rejection. This may happen consciously or subconsciously.

When this occurs, the same part of the brain that experiences physical pain is activated. Your brain is unable to differentiate between the sensation of physical and emotional pain, it just experiences pain.

By simply shifting your focus to the person talking, looking them in the eye and engaging in the conversation fully, you are sending messages to the other person's brain that you are not a threat to them or rejecting them in any way. You are showing respect and fairness to the other person and receiving the same in return.

3. Listen to understand

Most of us know when someone isn't truly listening to us. It drives us nuts!

But one of the biggest issues, which leads to miscommunication errors and missed connection, is that we listen to *speak*, not listen to *understand* another's point of view.

In *Deep Listening: Impact Beyond Words*, Oscar Trimboli explains:

> *"Research shows that most people only speak at 125 words per minute, but our mind can process 400 words per minute. There is a considerable gap between what they want to say and what they are actually saying."*

So most of the time, we are listening to answer back, to keep the dialogue going. However, if we were to slow down and avoid interrupting, we would give other people the chance to open up and communicate further, and deeper. When you do this, you really start to connect with people and get to the guts of the matter at hand.

Trimboli says we can dig deeper into the topic by asking a simple question "Is there anything else you would like to say, but haven't?".

It's when we start listening to the unsaid things that we start to transform our relationships for the better.

4. Share common ground

Finding things in common with people who you work with goes a long way to building trust. When you have things in common with people you establish rapport and build connection. Connection creates trust.

A simple exercise I do with clients is, in pairs, ask them to find five things they have in common with each other that aren't visibly obvious (e.g. arms, legs, ears, etc). During the exercise the energy in the room always changes, the noise level increases, laughter increases, people are smiling, connecting.

You can do this exercise with anyone, anytime and without being obvious about it. Through simply being curious and showing interest in someone you will start to find these commonalities. It puts new meaning into the value of small talk!

5. Be vulnerable

In his book *The Five Dysfunctions of a Team: A leadership fable*, Patrick Lencioni talks about using vulnerability to create trust by teams being able to talk about "weaknesses, skill deficiencies, interpersonal shortcomings, mistakes, and requests for help."

By creating trust within the team, people are then able to focus more on what needs to be achieved, by whom and by when, rather than on more self-serving activities.

We'll discuss vulnerability in more detail in the next chapter.

The cost of not building trust is significantly high, both in terms of money and energy, which impacts the overall culture and function of the organisation.

It's hard to be soft

The advantages of establishing and maintaining trust in organisations is well documented. In a study completed in 2003, Salamon found a positive relationship between employees who felt trusted and increased productivity, sales, shareholder and customer satisfaction and lower absenteeism. If you are only interested in the bottom line return, there it is.

But what about the intangible rewards of trust? For example, being liked as a person, being respected, having a good reputation and being inspiring as a leader are all benefits.

Some consider trust to be a soft skill of leadership, however, I would argue that it's harder to do the soft stuff than it is to do the day-to-day running of a business. Not everyone is comfortable building relationships with other people, and I've heard many people say that they actively avoid going to social or networking events at work because they have to talk to other people!

Additionally, many of us would rather be very transactional in our work conversations than take any additional time to get to know those we work with. It's easier, shows less of ourselves, saving us the risk of potential exposure to our vulnerabilities in case we are ridiculed or laughed at. Such is our need to protect ourselves.

By building trust, people will naturally want to follow you, work for you and strive for you. Your job will become easier because you will have the ability to influence more, both inside and outside of your remit, and you will feel more satisfied with what you are achieving. You will be able to get things done quicker and cheaper and create stability for your people.

Creativity, innovation and possibility all become high potency variables within your world when built on trust.

Wouldn't you say that's worth the investment?

Five years to build; fine minutes to destroy

Susan felt a little overwhelmed about the work she was asked to do. She had done something similar in the past, and it had all worked out well, but this was a little different, and she felt unsure about it.

After agonising over it for a few hours, she thought the best course of action would be to talk to her boss, Melissa. Susan was confident that if nothing else Melissa would be able to point her in the right direction.

Melissa had always told Susan to come to her if she had any problems or questions as she was happy to help. So Susan organised to meet with Melissa specifically to discuss the work.

When they met, Susan went through the information as she had planned and outlined what she thought would be a possible solution. Susan had some quite specific questions about what she felt was missing from the brief about the work, and asked Melissa her first question.

Melissa replied, "Why are you asking me this? I would have thought that for someone at your level in the organisation, you would have come across this type of thing before and be able to get it done. If you can't manage it, perhaps I should take it off you and do it myself? In fact, I think that might be the best way to get this done. Hand over what you have done and I will look after it from here."

Susan felt like she had been slapped in the face. All the trust that she had for Melissa up to that conversation had disappeared. Susan felt disappointed, horrified and betrayed. What was previously a relationship based on mutual respect and trust had disintegrated in the space of a five-minute conversation.

The next day Susan started looking for a job.

By questioning Susan's ability to do her job, instead of focusing on the issue at hand, Melissa damaged the trust that Susan had in her. Melissa showed little respect for how Susan was feeling. By questioning her ability to do the job and taking over the work from Susan she showed through her actions that she had little trust in Susan being able to get the job done.

She stifled Susan's ability to think creatively about solving the problem and also did not follow through on what she had always said about coming to her with any problems or questions. The final cost was that Melissa lost a good employee and will now waste money recruiting her replacement.

Words to practise trust

- 'I'm sorry, I've never done that before.'
- 'I was wrong because…'
- 'I learned that the hard way.'
- 'I would like to have an open and honest conversation with you about…'
- 'How are you coping with everything? What can I help you with?'
- 'How has your past experience helped you to manage this?'
- 'I accept accountability for what has gone wrong here.'
- 'What could I have done differently to help?'

Actions to practise trust

- Do what you say you will do, always. If you need to change your mind say so and explain why, so people understand.
- Show vulnerability by admitting if you don't know something, you've made a mistake or by asking for help when you need it.
- Share stories of situations where something has gone wrong and you've learned from it.
- Tell people something personal about yourself (always within reason and with respect).
- Look for commonalities with people by being curious and asking questions (again with respect and within reason).

- Be open and honest and truthful, always with respect and kindness.
- Respectfully let people know where they stand with you, with integrity.
- Share accountability for the good, bad and the ugly.

Behaviours to practise trust

- Are you often let down by those you work with? Or do you let them down?
- Do you trust your peers that they will do what they say they will or are they always doing the opposite?
- Will your boss always be there to support you even if you make a big fat hairy mistake?
- Are you angry or upset when your team makes a mistake, and do you let them know?
- Do you give people the benefit of the doubt?
- Do you know your people well and understand what they are experiencing in their personal lives?

Chapter 8

I CAN BE VULNERABLE

As he sat at the table in front of the camera with tears streaming down his face, our hearts broke for him. His devastation at what he had done was palpable and his regret and sorrow written all over his face. As the cameras clicked and bulbs flashed he stared down, clearly wishing he was somewhere, anywhere, but here. The room was cold and filled with expectation for answers. The press demanded answers. Their viewers and readers demanded answers. His manager and father stood behind him off to the right, clearly saddened and equally distressed. The situation was grave, tense and heart-breaking.

As captain of the Australian cricket team, Steve Smith was vulnerable that day, and by letting the world see his pain, he may well have won back the respect of many people both within and outside the cricketing community. His ability to recognise and acknowledge that his very own leadership had led to the situation that let down his team, his family and his country was testament to the great leader that he was, and still is.

On 24th March 2018, during the third test against South Africa, Australian cricketer Cameron Bancroft was observed by television cameras rubbing the ball with a small yellow item, later determined to be sand paper. When inspected by the ground referee there was no clear evidence that the ball was indeed altered in any way, and play resumed.

At the conclusion of play that day, at the post-match press conference, Bancroft and captain Smith admitted to using a small piece of adhesive with grit attached to create an abrasive surface on the ball. Following an investigation by Cricket Australia, Smith admitted that the adhesive was sandpaper, a common tool used to roughen their bats. Smith also admitted that the plan had been concocted by the "leadership group" of the team and that he was well aware of the plan ahead of its implementation.

What followed has been called a dark day for Australian cricket. The condemnation that resulted from everyone from the Australian Prime Minister through to the parents who officiate backyard cricket, was nothing short of phenomenal. There was scathing criticism from past and present players and sympathy and empathy from those who have possibly walked in Smith's shoes before, and understand the shame and humiliation of making such an error in judgment. And finally, the dissection and analysis of every vantage point of the event by the press for weeks on end, ensured that the Australian public were all included as judge and jury.

So, what happened?

Just 12 months earlier, Steve Smith had been celebrated for reaching his 50th test match. He was considered to be "a leader of men that's never been afraid to take on a challenge" and "a player with supreme confidence in his ability". He was at the top of his game, in the finest of form and in complete control of a very positive future. He probably never expected that this would be the toughest experience he would ever face in his leadership career. He would need all his courage and strength to manage this challenge.

Leaders make mistakes – but you have to be completely and absolutely accountable for them and be vulnerable enough to own up and apologise for them.

Weakness or strength?

Remember when you were a child and were told not to cry, to be brave and occasionally to 'suck it up sunshine'? The ability to be vulnerable is beaten out of us at an early age. In particular, men are taught in society that they shouldn't show emotion, let alone cry in front of another human being.

Brene Brown, author of books such as *Daring Greatly* and *The Power of Vulnerability*, has dedicated her career to researching this topic. She believes that vulnerability is not a weakness, but in fact a measure of courage.

How much courage does it take to stand in front of someone and admit you've made a mistake or failed at something, and then ask for forgiveness, a re-grouping, a new path forward to follow? If we ask Steve Smith that question I expect he would nod, knowingly.

The reason this is so powerful is because we have all been there and can all relate to how it feels. Most of us are able to stand in another person's shoes and feel their discomfort, and when we do the connection between us is instantly formed because we feel their pain, physically and mentally.

Brene Brown goes so far as to say that vulnerability is the mother of innovation – without the vulnerability of failure, true innovation and creativity cannot occur.

Vulnerability is a very underestimated leadership quality that many still incorrectly see as a weakness.

Connection creation

As humans, we are designed to crave and create connection with others. It is this that makes us feel part of a tribe or family. Stemming from the prehistoric era, when we faced life or death situations on a daily basis, we created tribes as a safety net to ensure our survival. We learned from one another, taught each other skills and learned to adapt and evolve into the human race as we know it now. Some would argue this hasn't necessarily panned out in the best way possible, but hope reigns eternal as we continue to evolve, building tribes, families and communities.

When we are surrounded by our loved ones and feel part of a collective group, personally or professionally, science says our brains produce two chemicals. The first is oxytocin, a peptide hormone produced by the hypothalamus and released by the posterior pituitary gland which plays a role in social bonding, helping us to make a connection.

The second is dopamine, a chemical of the catecholamine and phenethylamine families responsible for the feeling we get when we have done a great job and feel good about it, making us more motivated. Our brains are in constant pursuit of these chemicals, we crave them and at times get addicted to them. (Ask any researcher, gym junky or professional athlete.)

When we are not part of a family or group, are feeling on the outer or being alienated by others, our body produces a chemical called cortisol. Cortisol is produced when we are stressed, fearful or under pressure; it is produced by the adrenal gland. It has a shelf life in our body of about 72 hours, hence when our lives are missing that connection with others, we live with a body that continues to develop cortisol which can lead to conditions like anxiety and depression.

As a human race, we need to connect with people to ensure our survival. In a work context, we often see that highly successful teams and organisations have a leader who creates this connection. Nobody does anything alone, ever. There is usually a tribe, a family, a team behind everyone who achieves something successful.

You need people, people need you. Achievement or innovation in isolation is impossible.

A fine line

Don't get me wrong, I'm not suggesting for one minute that you need to expose your inner secrets and cry uncontrollably in front of a work colleague to practise being vulnerable.

Things like asking for help, sharing your personal story, saying that you don't know the answer to something, or being open to and accepting of challenge from others, all require a level of vulnerability yet they are somewhat easier to do.

Sometimes you have to stand alone, speak the loudest or fight hard for what you believe in, which requires equal parts strength, courage and vulnerability.

Being vulnerable means walking a fine line between overuse and underuse, as Figure 8.1 shows.

Figure 8.1: Overuse versus underuse

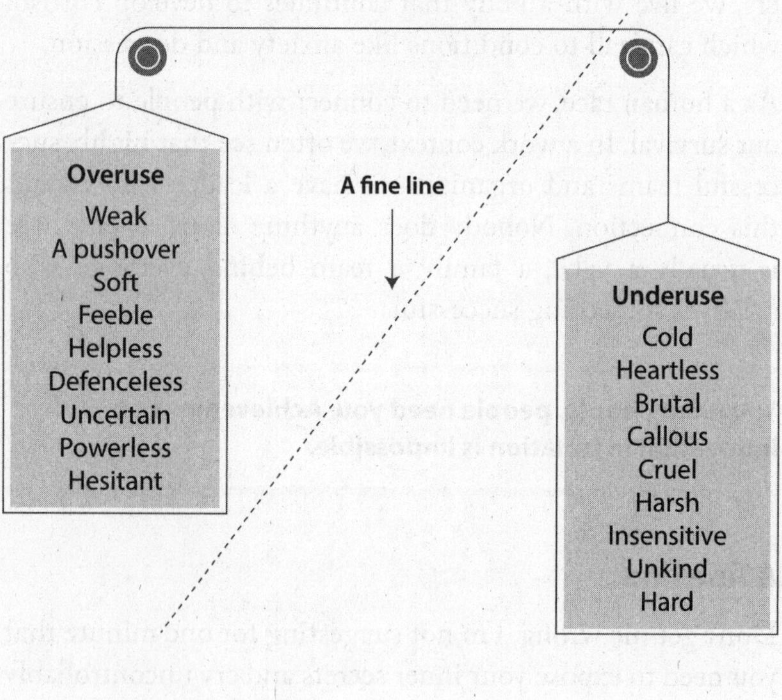

Overuse versus underuse

The overuse of vulnerability can potentially undermine your strength and have the opposite effect of its value, resulting in a lack of confidence from those you lead. It can make you look like a pushover, defenceless, helpless and hesitant, all things that cancel out the work you have done to show your strength.

You should never use your vulnerability to manipulate or engineer a situation to your favour, or you'll demonstrate to everyone that you can't be trusted.

On the other hand, underuse of vulnerability can result in people being considered cold, calculating, heartless and insensitive. Some would argue what we have these qualities in abundance in our corporate environment already!

For men, this is particularly relevant as society trains our boys from a young age not to show or feel any emotion. Women, however, are perceived as showing too much vulnerability or emotion and can often be considered too soft. Then again, if they don't show any vulnerability (especially in business), they are thought of as insensitive, heartless or an 'Ice Queen'. It's no win for us girls!

There is a fine line to over and under using vulnerability and a good gauge is to consider two things:

1. Is your intention positive or negative?

2. Are you trying to create a connection with someone?

If you have a positive intention and are trying to build a connection, you can do so quite effectively with vulnerability because you are increasing the level of understanding and empathy.

For example, a leader I once worked with was trying to motivate his team for the last three months of their financial year, to keep going even though it felt hard. The leader enjoyed running marathons in his spare time, so he spoke to the team about the process he goes through when running a marathon, and how mentally he is fine up until the last quarter of the run.

During this time, his head starts to tell him how tired he is, how painful his legs are, how easy it would be to stop. He then needs to find the strength inside to keep going, which is always hard. His team, while not marathon runners themselves, were able to understand and empathise with him through his vulnerability.

If your intention for being vulnerable is to influence someone for the wrong reasons, you risk being perceived as inauthentic and manipulative.

Research completed by Professor Paula Niedenthal of the University of Wisconsin-Madison shows that our brains take in large amounts of biographical data on the state of people we are observing, for example, facial expression, demeanour, body language, etc. This process is done subconsciously and is called resonance, or how we resonate with someone.

A simple example of this is when someone smiles at you and it's not a genuine smile. You can instantly detect it's not genuine. However, when someone smiles at you, even a stranger on the street, and it's genuine you will usually smile back. Because our brains are constantly looking for connection, when we pick up markers of inauthenticity, it's like a warning signal. So, tread carefully and genuinely with vulnerability.

Accept the challenge

So, what are some ways that we can learn or practise the language of vulnerability?

Ask for pushback

I once coached a leader who actively encouraged his people to challenge him without fear of retribution or repercussions when they disagreed with him. At times, he even admitted he may have got it wrong and that it could have been done better/different. By accepting challenge from his team, this leader empowered his team to be courageous and show strength (by challenging), while he was being vulnerable (by showing he didn't always get it right).

Encourage opportunities to personally connect

I often run an exercise with leadership teams where each person brings a personal item to work and talks about what it means to them, to the team. This creates a level of vulnerability without getting too deep and personal, because each person can share as much or as little as they would like to. This is a great opportunity to step into another person's shoes, understand more about them as a whole person, and show empathy and understanding towards them.

Talk about your mistakes

I've seen a leader talk about an experience he had when managing a situation that didn't go very well and what he learned from that experience. This helped the team to see that they were on the same path and showed them what to watch out for along the way.

A similar example of this is the CEO of United Airlines in the US who had tried to implement a new performance management plan across the airline. The plan wasn't received well and there was significant backlash from employees. The CEO then sent an email to all employees admitting that he had got it wrong, and that they were going to withdraw the plan based on employee feedback.

Ask for help

Early in my career I worked for a leader who asked me if I could help him out on a piece of work that he had never done before. We spoke about his plans about he was to go about completing it, his thoughts on what the risks were and how he could mitigate them along the way. It was as if I was coaching him on how to do it and I felt pretty chuffed he had asked me. It was nice to know that he didn't have all the answers and that it wasn't beneath him to ask for help. As a result, the experience made our relationship stronger.

You don't need to pour your heart out to people to be vulnerable, just sharing a little more of your story goes a long way.

Risky business

By admitting that you don't have all the answers, you show those you work with that you are vulnerable enough to own this, in turn creating an environment and culture that is open to sharing and building on ideas. This leads to greater buy-in from your people through their active participation in solving problems.

People become more empowered and engaged as they create more certainty around themselves. They build respect for themselves and each other and a safer environment for raising issues and problems resulting in improved risk management. Those working for you are less likely to leave, more likely to give you their discretionary effort and will achieve far more than working alone.

Being vulnerable is risky, because it makes you *feel* – something many of us have long forgotten how to do. Feelings make us exposed. You have to acknowledge something inside that in all likelihood you have ignored for a long time. It's uncomfortable, it's raw, it's scary.

But it's also liberating, refreshing and insightful. And if you are going to learn something today, it may as well be about yourself. Like courage, feeling stuff can be practised and the more you expose yourself to it, the more comfortable you become with doing it.

Feeling vulnerable gives you the opportunity to not be so 'together' all the time, to let go of control and to lean into the release of the pressure of having to know everything, be everything and have everything.

When we are vulnerable and create connection with those we work for and with, we are better able to influence and inspire.

Help is at hand

Sarah worked for a man she despised. When the job was new, he seemed to give her lots of space to do her job, welcomed her new ideas and fresh perspective, and involved her in lots of the decision making for the team. Then things changed.

Sarah now felt that he was an arrogant, self-serving man who didn't seem interested in anything that she had to say, let alone listen to any of her many ideas for improving the function. So, she started to put her feelers out for a new job. She didn't feel as though she could sustain working for him for much longer.

To make things worse, things at home were hectic. Her husband was travelling a lot, leaving her to manage their two children on her own. She pinged between dropping the kids off to school and day care, getting to work late, leaving early to collect them, and logging back on to work in the evening to catch up on the work hours she had missed. Her mother was also sick, having recently been diagnosed with Type 2 Diabetes, and Sarah seemed to be spending a lot of her time helping her mother to understand how to best manage this. Sarah's father had died some years ago and her sister lived interstate, so the majority of her mother's care was left up to her.

Sarah was a good communicator, always trying to keep the lines of communication active with her stakeholders, peers and boss so she thought that she had better let her boss know that she was a little bit off this week due to so much going on at home. When she rang her boss to let him know, he seemed sympathetic and suggested that they catch up for a coffee later in the day, to which she agreed.

They met at the coffee shop around the corner from work and she could feel his mood wasn't good from the moment she sat down.

"Sarah," he said, "I want to talk to you about how you manage things at home."

"Sure," she replied, while thinking "here it comes" and wondering what great "advice" she was going to get from him, since he clearly thought she wasn't coping enough to be able to manage home and work.

"I need your help because I'm not coping at all." As he started to tear up he added, "I separated from my wife six months ago and have been trying to get settled in a new house and manage our five-year-old child. I don't think I'm doing a good job so wanted to get your advice".

Sarah's perception of her boss changed in an instant. She now understood more about his situation and that the façade he had been portraying at work, had really been to hide his pain. She reached for his hand and gave it a squeeze and said, "I'd be happy to help, however I can."

They connected as trusted colleagues that day, through his ability to be vulnerable and ask her for help and her deeper understanding of his world. She also stopped looking for a job, and decided hers wasn't so bad after all.

Words to practise vulnerability

- 'I'm sorry…'
- 'I've never been in this situation before…'
- 'Forgive me for…'
- 'I'm not really sure…'
- 'Let's explore that together.'
- 'I learned a valuable lesson from…'
- 'Thanks so much for that.'
- 'I really value what you have done.'

Actions to practise vulnerability

- Say sorry for something you did or forgot to do.
- Admit your weaknesses.
- Share stories of when you have failed at something and what you learned from it.
- Own up when you don't know something.
- Be open minded about everything.
- Suspend your judgment.
- Say thank you, always.

Behaviours to practise vulnerability

- Do you share personal stories with your team and do you know theirs?
- Do you ask for help, or do your people feel comfortable to ask you for help?
- Do you accept the advice of those who report to you?

- Do you admit to your people that you don't have all the solutions or do you feel obliged to have all the answers?
- Do you admit when you get it wrong and accept accountability in front of others, or do you never get it wrong?

Part III

PRACTISE THE BEHAVIOUR

Like most things in life, each of the six languages you've just learned have some risks. If you underuse them, you could be deemed too weak; overuse them and you're too hard.

Having the knowledge, understanding and practical ability to apply each language when and where it is needed is key to getting the most out of them. It really is a bit of a juggling act!

Remember that as leaders we are always in a glaring spotlight in front of our people, colleagues and boss, and we are constantly being judged on what we say and what we do.

Like actors in a play, learning and rehearsing is part of using the languages of leadership so that we become better at them in front of our audience. Always use them with positive intention, for the greater good of the organisation, and with great care and consideration for everyone involved.

Part III will help you with that.

Chapter 9

I CAN BALANCE THE ACT

Holly Graf was the first American woman to captain a US Navy Cruiser. She had come from fine naval stock, her father was also a captain, her sister a rear admiral, and her brother-in-law an admiral. Considered to be high potential she held a number of officer positions before being promoted to captain in 2007 and then commanding officer of the USS Cowpens in March 2008.

Holly was fiercely determined, highly ambitious and brilliant at sea with a long and decorated career including being awarded honours such as the Legion of Merit and the Bronze Star. As part of her service, she participated in Operation Iraqi Freedom in 2003.

Yet, on 13 January 2010, Captain Graf was relieved of her captaincy following an investigation into her behaviour of cruelty and maltreatment of the crew and conduct unbecoming an officer during her time on the Cowpens. The investigation resulted after many allegations from crew members of physical and verbal abuse aboard the ship.

The environment aboard the Cowpens was described as "an environment of fear and hostility" due to many expletive ridden rants, verbal and physical assaults and demeaning and humiliating behaviour by Captain Graf towards the crew. The crew developed nicknames for her along the lines of The Sea Witch, Horrible Holly and Miss Bligh (in reference to Captain Bligh of Mutiny on the Bounty). Her leadership created a culture of fear and aggression on board, and it appears this was not an isolated instance.

Graf apparently had a long history of poor behaviour towards her subordinates. She was renowned for yelling, spitting at and bullying her crew. During her time as captain of the USS Winston S. Churchill, between April 2002 and February 2004, the ship's chaplain reported the crew's morale as being the lowest he had ever seen in his 20-year naval career. She was known to spit at people and throw things like coffee cups and binders when she was annoyed. When she was ultimately relieved of her command the crew broke out in cheers of joy.

Captain Graf was clearly a strong woman who deserved, through the hard work and dedication throughout her career, to be in the position she was in as captain. Where she went wrong was the overuse of her strength to the point of destroying the culture of the ship and her personal and professional reputation as a sea captain. The consequences of her actions were to create a poor culture within the teams that she led, and ultimately the demise of her role as captain.

She has influenced so many lives in the Navy, sadly in the wrong way.

The most powerful tool any leader has is their words, actions and behaviours – how you use them counts.

Set your speed

Each of the languages that we have covered in Part II can be overused and underused, which results in significantly different outcomes.

The aim is to be able to identify the situation and use the relevant language as part of your overall leadership tool kit. If you use any of the languages too much, you may find yourself in a similar situation to Captain Graf – doing damage to the fragile relationships that you manage on a day-to-day basis with those you lead, those you work with and those you report to.

Balancing each language well, depends on the circumstances surrounding its use. Think of it like a speedometer in your car (see Figure 9.1 overleaf). If you go too slowly, you take too long to get where you need to be. So, if you don't use a language when you need to, you may be too late and not get the right outcome.

Alternatively, if you are too fast, your driving becomes dangerous and you take risks, possibly not arriving at your destination (or arriving in a terrible state!). If you overuse each language you put at risk your reputation, your team's engagement and you definitely won't take people on the right journey.

The aim is to balance your speed within the required limit, so you arrive safely, with everyone on board and happy.

Figure 9.1: Language speedometer

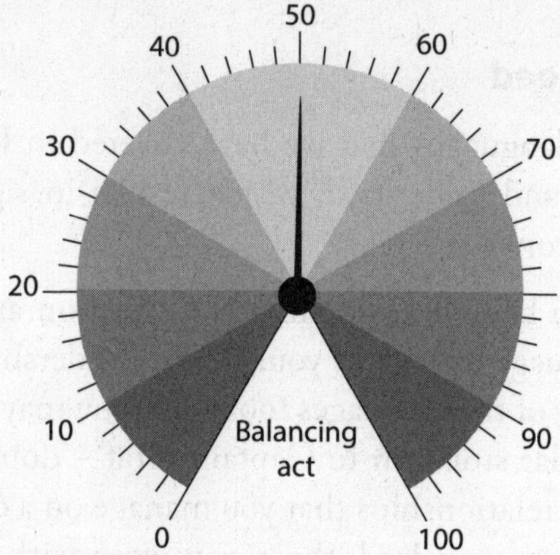

Using each language within your limits, when required, will bring those around you on a relatively smooth ride.

Let's look at what happens when you're too fast or too slow in each of the languages.

I am courageous

Being too courageous can lead to getting a reputation as a cowboy. Taking too many risks, even if they pay off, invariably leads to an environment of arrogance, ego and greed.

The 2004 rogue trader scandal at the National Australia Bank, where four currency traders lost $360 million because they continued to take too many risks, was a perfect example of being too courageous. The impact of their actions on their employer, their colleagues, their families and their lives resulted in a complete loss of trust and respect.

On the reverse of this, not being courageous enough (or at all) may reduce your ability to get anything done.

Being too scared of risk keeps you treading water, not being able to shift anything or anyone.

Keeping the status quo will reduce innovation and creativity within your business, limiting those around you to think outside of the box and come up with different ways of doing things. You will become stagnant, mundane and quickly outdated. You may also become very boring!

I am strong

As we have seen with Captain Graf, the overuse of strength can result in you being viewed as a 'hard-arse', a bully and someone who no-one wants to work with or for. You will build a reputation as too difficult to work with, and people will resent you and dislike you for the wrong reasons.

Make no mistake, throughout your leadership career you will be disliked by some, not everyone is liked all the time. But there is a difference between being disliked for being a nasty, insensitive and heartless person, and being disliked yet respected because you are tough but fair and respectful to others.

On the other hand, if you aren't strong enough, you can be perceived as a pushover, weak and not an inspirational leader. This will put at risk the respect those around you have for you, or that you can earn in the future.

I recall being in a situation where a senior leader was trying to shut down the work I was doing because he felt it was encroaching on his space. He was perceived as a highly political person within the organisation I was working, and my boss at the time let him shut down what I was working on. I felt completely let down by the fact that my leader didn't support me and stand up to this person.

As long as politics and political people continue to be allowed to reign in organisations, we will continue to lose good people, good time and good money due to the havoc they cause.

As a leader you need to show your strength and lead the way.

I engineer the world around me

When you over-engineer things, you can be perceived as manipulative and political, particularly when engineering for the wrong reasons. You will also spend a lot of your time engineering situations to occur, which will over-complicate things and potentially use up all your time and energy.

Being labelled as a political player is never good for your brand. You are perceived as self-centred, egotistical and narcissistic – all things to be avoided in the world of being a great leader.

I worked with a woman once who spent the majority of her work day moving things around, as if we were all on a chess table. She would sit at her desk and watch as things played out, always ready to jump in and save the day right at the most appropriate time. She was eventually dismissed for causing too much disruption and never getting any work done.

When we don't engineer things for our team, we can earn a reputation of being uncaring or uninterested in the development of our people.

Everyone needs to take an active role in their own development. However, finding situations to stretch and develop are not always as obvious to others as they are to you. You also have a broader stretch across different functions and teams, enabling you to better identify alternative solutions.

To not put our people into situations that stretch and develop them is running the risk of losing their respect, their interest and their engagement in work.

I abdicate responsibility to others

We have all worked with leaders who are guilty of over-delegating the work they are responsible for, becoming lazy, lethargic and indifferent. These types of leaders have all but given up, they are unmotivated and really just filling up a position usually waiting for a golden handshake out of the organisation. As they sit in the chair, they cause a ripple effect throughout the organisation because other people are unable to move up into the position they are holding.

Leaders above them are usually unwilling to move them on or performance-manage them because they do just enough to get them through, or the people working for them are doing a great job meeting the deliverables required to sustain their employment.

This leads to disempowered people, low creativity, engagement and innovation. People become more stressed and overworked trying to keep up with it all, and fostering a culture of distrust, fear and uncertainty. It also takes away people's curiosity and their responsibility. They don't need to be accountable for anything because this now sits with you. You create a 'them and us' mentality, and a culture of blame and fear. It's a long way back from that.

When you don't abdicate you become a control freak, unable to let go of things, to let others make decisions and to give up ownership of work.

I trust and am trusted

Like abdication, when you don't trust someone you increase your need for control and people will resent you for it. Once you don't trust someone, you need to be across far more detail than if you were working within a trusting relationship.

Similar to when you don't abdicate, you create a team of people who are disempowered, unhappy and uncertain. This all affects your bottom line through high turnover, lower profits and increased expenses.

Being overly trustful of people may also come at a cost. Putting your trust in people who have not earned it, may result in disappointment, and potential loss of profit and income. In all cases, people should earn your trust and you should earn theirs.

When someone loses your trust, you should draw on your strength to let them know. This gives them the opportunity to either earn it back or let it go, and it offers you great insight into the person you are dealing with.

Trust mustn't be given freely, as this diminishes its value.

I can be vulnerable

Finally, when you are too vulnerable you may be perceived as weak, scared to take risks and potentially not knowing what you are doing.

We attribute people's behaviour to a flaw in their personality and not the circumstances or environment in which they are in. Therefore, you will be judged by those around you, and usually judged harshly. By showing too much vulnerability too often, you will be perceived as having no strength, and you will lose the confidence in your leadership from your people.

On the reverse, not showing any vulnerability will lead people to believe you are cold, heartless and uncaring about those around you.

A little vulnerability goes a long way, so use it wisely and always with good intentions of building trust and relationships with those around you.

Showcase your skills

A colleague of mine some years ago made a comment that has stayed with me for many years. One afternoon we were talking about a workshop that was being run for senior leaders, which had its foundations in acting. Her comment to me was "Perhaps all of our leaders should take acting lessons, so they can at least act like they care about their people!". We laughed at the time, but it has stuck with me. Here's why.

As leaders we are always on show. Regardless of where and when we are, someone in our organisation is watching what we are doing and what we are saying. This puts enormous pressure on us to get things right, all the time. Add to this the nature of today's society where we are judged immediately and hung out to dry as some kind of living example of the latest cause, if we say or do something against popular opinion.

Today more than ever, people feel they have the right to judge and assess based on their morals and values, and then say so as loudly as possible via any electronic means available. It's no wonder nobody wants to take any risks or say/do anything differently.

So, like actors in a play, we need to be word perfect, doing the right things at the right time, always in full view of our audience.

In the 1970s, Noel Burch from Gordon Training International developed the Four Stages of Learning model that helps us understand how we master any new skill.

As actors learn and rehearse their scenes they move back and forth through these same four levels of learning:

1. You don't know that you don't know something, so by not understanding or knowing how to do it, you are **unconsciously incompetent** at it.
2. You become aware that you don't know it and become **consciously incompetent** as you start to learn the new skill.
3. You then shift to **consciously competent** as you are learning, then the new skill becomes set in your brain.
4. You now don't have to think about it anymore, so you become **unconsciously competent.**

So, when you learn to use the languages of leadership, you need to start being consciously incompetent, practising and using each language until you eventually become unconsciously competent. You can do this through rehearsing each language to become better at it.

For example, when you want to be more vulnerable you can practise using your personal stories from your past, so that when you need to draw on them your brain is so familiar with the lines you need to say. Or when you want to be strong and stand up for what you believe in, if you have practised the phrases to use, it becomes easier.

Talking through different scenarios and situations with colleagues and friends in a safe and secure environment helps you to shift from conscious incompetence through to conscious competence, until you have practised them enough they become built into your unconscious memory.

Remember that, like all things you practise to become good at, it requires focus and commitment to build the skill.

Practice makes perfect

When we start out using a new skill, we need to be consciously aware of building that skill as we learn to master it. Along the learning journey, it often feels uncomfortable and automated, and you really need to apply focus to getting it right. This is normal and can often feel like you are overdoing it all the time. Don't worry and stick with it.

Like all good actors, knowing your lines and moves as much as possible provides you with the security that you will get there in the end, and the occasional slip up then becomes easily forgivable.

It is a fine balancing act to use the six languages of leadership. It's an act that should be taken seriously and with positive intent to avoid over or under usage. In their extremes, they are all detrimental to your leadership ability and will lead to the creation of a culture that isn't conducive to achievement and excellence.

When used wisely and at the right time the benefits to your culture, your achievements and your leadership legacy will be lasting and sustainable.

FINAL WORDS

The ability to influence and create an impression on those you work with, so that they want to do work with you and for you, is a constant aspiration for good leaders. After all, if you could master this, then getting work done would be easier for you, wouldn't it?

As a leader you should always be looking for ways to have an impact on those around you, or the situation that presents to you.

Having this type of impact is evident in those among us who are considered to be great leaders. It's that 'thing' they have that sets them apart from others. For example, Barack Obama, Angela Merkel and Oprah Winfrey all have great influence and gravitas, often leading the way with seeming ease and style.

So, pause for a minute and consider:

- How can you impact those around you the most?
- How do you want your leadership to impact those you work with or the organisation that you work for?

Your impact is your leadership footprint.

Long after you have moved on to another role or organisation, your team, colleagues and your boss will remember the impact that you had on them and their career.

When you think about those leaders who have left a lasting impression on you, what was their impact, both good and bad? And how do you make sure that the impact you leave on people is good and you have made them feel they were at their best when they worked with you?

Maya Angelou said, "People will forget what you said, people will forget what you did, but people will never forget how you made them feel". The opportunity for you as a leader is to use what you say and what you do to help people to feel valued, energised and engaged.

When you are *courageous* and standing up for what you believe in, people become inspired to do the same. They see in you a willingness to not accept the status quo and they see your effort to try to change things for the better.

Showing *strength* shows others that you have conviction in your leadership and you stand by what you say and do. You are fair, respectful and fully understand your purpose and values and these guide your decisions and judgements.

By understanding your environment, and being able to view situations from different perspectives, you are best able to *engineer* a situation to get the most out of it for everyone involved. You can determine and understand what drives those around you to create mutually beneficial relationships.

You can truly empower those around you by stepping back and *abdicating* responsibility and accountability while being fully supportive. Remember that empowering people is 50%

letting them own it and 50% you letting go. This isn't an easy thing to do and will require your strength and courage, trust and vulnerability.

Trusting and being *trusted* form the foundation of all the relationships that we manage, both personally and professionally, so working on maintaining that trust will need to be top of mind. Ensuring that we show respect and fairness and that we are open and honest will help to strengthen and build trust in our relationships.

And finally, we come to *vulnerability* – showing others that we are human, we can make mistakes and that we don't always know everything, but we are willing to give things a go even if we fail. When we share ourselves with those around us we create connection, build work families and achieve great things, together.

These languages show you how to use your words, actions and behaviours to have a positive, lasting experience with those you work with, those you lead and those you report to.

I received a call from a client I worked with last year. We had been focusing on developing the languages that he felt he needed to work on the most – strength, courage and trust.

Throughout that work he confronted some very real issues for him, which we worked at persistently, using the words and actions in each chapter. His ultimate aim was to get to a more senior role within the organisation he worked for, to lead a larger team, and to trust in his own ability to be able to do the job.

He rang me to tell me that he had got the promotion he wanted and that he couldn't have done it without doing the hard work we had done together. Overall, he felt more confident going into this role than he had about going to any other role he had held previously.

Now you know the languages of leadership, you can become an active, perceptive and directive leader, like my client. You too can develop your leadership languages to be the best you can be and to achieve what you set out to do. Through practice and commitment, nothing in this book is outside of your reach. You really just need to start.

As Body Shop founder Anita Roddick put it: "If you think you're too small to have an impact, try going to bed with a mosquito."

I know you can do great things.

Wendy

TALK TO ME

For me there is no greater reward for what I do than hearing from my clients that they have achieved what they set out to do, or that they are now working more effectively together, or even just that they have used one of the simple tools I have given them to great effect. This is why I do the work that I do.

If you would like to share with me your stories, good and not so good, about how the languages of leadership work for you, please get in touch. I'd love to hear from you.

You can find out more about me on my website wendyborn.com.au or you can contact me directly at wendy@wendyborn.com.au.

If you need further help I can tailor a coaching program or corporate leadership development package to you or your organisation specifically. I can also speak at your function or event, so please contact me for more information.

I truly hope this book helps you on your leadership journey, and that you enjoy reading it as much as I have enjoyed writing it.

I wish you all the very best in putting it into practice, and inspiring those around you as you do.

As Walt Disney famously said: "All our dreams come true, if we have the courage to pursue them."

Wendy

SOURCES

Chapter 1

Coombe, D. (2016) "Don't Take It Personally" Is Terrible Work Advice, *Harvard Business Review*, https://hbr.org/2016/03/dont-take-it-personally-is-terrible-work-advice

Building Workplace Trust Trends and High Performance, 2015 Interaction Associates Inc. http://interactionassociates.com/sites/default/files/research_items/Trust%20Report_2014_15IA_0.pdf

Covey, S. (2012) *The 7 Habits of Highly Effective People*, Simon & Schuster.

Goleman, D. (2007) *Emotional Intelligence*, Random House Inc.

Lebowitz, S. (2016) A 24-year-old who spent 10 days working in complete isolation discovered a key insight about productivity, *Business Insider Australia* https://www.businessinsider.com.au/why-relationships-are-the-key-to-productivity-20162?r=US&IR=T

Meier, C. and Dumani, S. (2015) in the *Journal of Organizational Behavior.*

Porter, J. (2017) Why you should make time for self-reflection (even if you hate doing it), *Harvard Business Review*, https://hbr.org/2017/03/why-you-should-make-time-for-self-reflection-even-if-you-hate-doing-it?autocomplete=true

Rath, T. (2006) *Vital Friends, The people you can't afford to live without*, Gallup Press.

Sherman, M. Ph.D. (2014) Why we don't give each other a break, *Psychology Today*, https://www.psychologytoday.com/au/blog/real-men-dont-write-blogs/201406/why-we-dont-give-each-other-break

Stefano, G.D., Gino, F., Pisano, G.P. and Staats, B.R. (2016) *Making Experience Count: The Role of Reflection in Individual Learning*, https://papers.ssrn.com/sol3/papers.cfm?abstract_id=2414478

Chapter 2

Couros, G. (2017) *The One Quality All Successful People Have*, https://georgecouros.ca/blog/archives/tag/where-focus-goes-energy-flows

Goleman, D. (2014) *The Well-Focused Leader*, http://www.europeanbusinessreview.com/the-well-focused-leader/

Lehrer, J. The Mirror Neuron Revolution: Explaining What Makes Humans Social, *Scientific American*, https://www.scientificamerican.com/article/the-mirror-neuron-revolut/

Taylor, Dr. J. (2014) Focus Is the Gateway to Business Success, https://www.huffingtonpost.com/dr-jim-taylor/focus-is-the-gateway-to-b_b_4206552.html

Chapter 3

Aldoa, A. Ph.D. (2014) *Why Labeling Emotions Matters*, https://www.psychologytoday.com/au/blog/sweet-emotion/201408/why-labeling-emotions-matters

Aman, J.L. (2013) *Five Reasons Fear Journals Benefit Mental Health,* https://www.healthyplace.com/blogs/anxiety-schmanxiety/2013/07/five-reasons-you-should-keep-a-fear-journal

Chua, C. *4 Reasons We should Overcome Fear,* https://personalexcellence.co/blog/fear/

Comaford, C. (2012) Hijack! How Your Brain Blocks Performance, https://www.forbes.com/sites/christinecomaford/2012/10/21/hijack-how-your-brain-blocks-performance/

Grohol, J.M. Psy.D. (2016) *What is Exposure Therapy?* https://psychcentral.com/lib/what-is-exposure-therapy/

Heath, C. & D. (2017) *The Power of Moments Why Certain Experiences Have Extraordinary Impact*, Simon & Schuster, New York.

PBS Series *Eyes on the Prize: America's Civil Rights Years* (1995) "Ain't Scared of Your Jails", https://www.youtube.com/watch?v=neDpuJVc4Ko

Rock, D. and Schwartz, J. (2006) *The Neuroscience of Leadership*, Booz & Company.

Serani, D. Psy.D. (2011) *If It Bleeds, It Leads: Understanding Fear-Based Media*, https://www.psychologytoday.com/au/blog/two-takes-depression/201106/if-it-bleeds-it-leads-understanding-fear-based-media

Smith, J. (2016) *How do Navy SEALs control their nerves?* https://www.quora.com/How-do-Navy-SEALs-control-their-nerves

Warrell, M., (2015) *Brave 50 Everyday Acts of Courage to Thrive in Work, Love and Life*, John Wiley & Sons Australia, Ltd.

Chapter 4

Heath, C. & D. (2017) *The Power of Moments Why Certain Experiences Have Extraordinary Impact*, Simon & Schuster, New York.

Heifetz, R.A. and Linsky, M. (2002) *Leadership on the Line Staying Alive through the Dangers of Leading*, Harvard Business School Publishing.

Lencioni, P, (2002) *The Five Dysfunctions of a Team – A Leadership Fable*, Jossey-Bass, San Francisco.

Morris, D. (2016) *5 Qualities of the Best Places to Work*, https://www.entrepreneur.com/article/272139

Sales, M. (2018) *The Power of Real Confidence – Learn How to Lead to Your Full Potential*, Major Street Publishing Pty Ltd, Highett.

Chapter 5

Caballero, M.C. (2004) Academic turns city into a social experiment, *The Harvard Gazette.*

Cohen, A.R. & Bradford, D.L. (2005) *Influence without Authority, 2nd Edition*, John Wiley & Sons, New Jersey.

Heath, C. and D. (2010) *Switch: How to change things when change is hard*, Broadway Books, New York.

Heifetz, R., Grashow, A. and Linsky, M. (2009) *The Practice of Adaptive Leadership, Tools and Tactics for Changing Your Organization and the World*, Harvard Business Review Press, Boston.

Heifetz, R.A. and Linsky, M. (2002) *Leadership on the Line Staying Alive through the Dangers of Leading*, Harvard Business Review Press, Boston.

Levin, M. (2017) *7 Reasons to Schedule Walking Meetings*, https://www.inc.com/marissa-levin/7-ways-walking-meetings-will-improve-your-companys-bottom-line.html

Marsh, S. (2013) *Antanas Mockus: Columbians fear ridicule more than being fined*, Global Public Leaders Network, *The Guardian.*

Merchant, N. (2013) *Got a meeting? Take a walk*, https://www.ted.com/talks/nilofer_merchant_got_a_meeting_take_a_walk

Posada, J., Ben-Michael, E., Herman, A., Kahan, E. and Richter, E. (2000*) Death and injury from motor vehicle crashes in Colombia*, Pan Am J Public Health.

Chapter 6

Brownlee, D. (2015) How to Handle The Four Most Common Types of Bad Bosses, https://www.fastcompany.com/3053062/how-to-handle-the-four-most-common-types-of-bad-bosses

Fern, M. MEd and Johnstone, M. Ph.D. (2005) *Holding On and Letting Go, Giving up control to become more powerful*, Vantage Point Consulting Pty Ltd.

Glasser, J. E. (2014) *Conversational Intelligence How Great Leaders Build trust and get Extraordinary Results*, Bibliomotion, Inc. Brookline.

Rock, D. and Schwartz, J. (2006) *The Neuroscience of Leadership*, Booz & Company.

Rock, D. (2009) Managing with the Brain in Mind, *Organizations & People*, Autumn 2009 Issue 56.

White, R.D. Jr., Ph.D., (2010) The Micromanagement Disease: Symptoms, Diagnosis, and Cure, *Public Personnel Management*, Vol. 39 No. 1.

Chapter 7

Allison, M. (2011) Costco's colourful CEO, co-founder Jim Sinegal to retire, *The Seattle Times.*

Brown, J. (2018) *Is social media bad for you? The evidence and the unknowns*, http://www.bbc.com/future/story/20180104-is-social-media-bad-for-you-the-evidence-and-the-unknowns

Brown, S., Gray, D., McHardy, J. and Taylor, K. (2015) Employee trust and workplace performance, *Journal of Economic Behavior & Organization* 116 (2015) 361 – 378.

Covey, S.M.R. and Conant D.R., (2016) The Connection Between Employee Trust and Financial Performance, *Harvard Business Review.*

Covey, S.M.R. (2007) *The Business Case for Trust*, https://chiefexecutive.net/the-business-case-for-trust/

Glasser, J. E. (2014) *Conversational Intelligence: How Great Leaders Build Trust and get Extraordinary Results*, Bibliomotion, Inc. Brookline.

Hitch, C. Ph.D. (2012) *How to Build Trust in an Organization*, UNC Kenan-Flagler Business School Executive Development.

Lencioni, P, (2002) *The Five Dysfunctions of a Team– A Leadership Fable*, Jossey-Bass, San Francisco.

Rock, D. and Schwartz, J. (2006) *The Neuroscience of Leadership*, Booz & Company.

Salamon, S.D. (2003) *Trust that Binds: The influence of collective felt trust on responsibility norms and organizational outcomes*, University of British Columbia.

Stallard, M. (2017) *Why Culture Makes Cosco America's Best Employer*, https://www.td.org/insights/why-culture-makes-costco-americas-best-employer

Trimboli, O. (2017) *Deep Listening: Impact beyond words.*

Chapter 8

ABC News (Australia) (2018) *Steve Smith breaks down during ball tampering press conference*, https://www.youtube.com/watch?v=HQBytgYVn0o

Brown, B. (2012) *Daring Greatly: How the Courage to be Vulnerable Transforms the Way We Live, Love, Parent and Lead*, Penguin Random House, New York.

Brown, B. (2012) *The Power of Vulnerability: Teachings on Authenticity, Connection & Courage*, Sounds True Inc, Louisville.

Caramela, S. (2018) *4 Ways to Unmask Vulnerability and Become a Stronger Leader*, https://www.businessnewsdaily.com/10680-unmasking-vulnerabilities-leadership.html

Haden, J. (2017) *To Be More Confident, Be More Vulnerable: 8 Counterintuitive Ways to Build Confidence*, https://www.inc.com/jeff-haden/to-be-more-confident-be-more-vulnerable-8-counterintuitive-ways-to-build-confide.html

News.com.au (2017) *'Harden up, you ****': The day a young Steve Smith proved his greatness*, https://www.news.com.au/sport/cricket/harden-up-you-the-day-a-young-steve-smith-proved-his-greatness/news-story/c83847074643f7a735c47ecf46e2d86a

Seppala, E. (2014) What Bosses Gain by Being Vulnerable, *Harvard Business Review*, https://hbr.org/2014/12/what-bosses-gain-by-being-vulnerable

Williams, D.K. (2013) *The Best Leaders are Vulnerable*, https://www.forbes.com/sites/davidkwilliams/2013/07/18/the-best-leaders-are-vulnerable/#6fcd39923c1d

Chapter 9

Adams, L. (2016) *Learning a New Skill is Easier Said Than Done, Gordon Training International*, http://www.gordontraining.com/free-workplace-articles/learning-a-new-skill-is-easier-said-than-done/

Allen, N. (2010) US Navy crew's mutiny against the 'Sea Witch' captain who 'belittled' them, *The Telegraph, UK* https://www.telegraph.co.uk/news/worldnews/northamerica/usa/7437034/US-Navy-crews-mutiny-against-the-Sea-Witch-captain-who--belittled-them.html

Heads roll at NAB over foreign exchange scandal, (2004) *The Sydney Morning Herald,* https://www.smh.com.au/business/heads-roll-at-nab-over-foreign-exchange-scandal-20040312-gdiizf.html

INDEX

Notes

Notes

Notes

Notes

Notes

Notes

Notes